HOW TO
HELP PEOPLE
CHANGE

Resources by Jay E. Adams

The Christian Counselor's Manual
The Christian Counselor's Casebook
Competent to Counsel
Handbook of Church Discipline
How to Help People Change
Marriage, Divorce, and Remarriage in the Bible
Preaching with Purpose
Shepherding God's Flock
Solving Marriage Problems
A Theology of Christian Counseling

HOW TO HELP PEOPLE CHANGE

The Four-Step Biblical Process

JAY E. ADAMS

ZONDERVAN™

GRAND RAPIDS, MICHIGAN 49530 USA

ZONDERVAN™

How to Help People Change
Copyright © 1986 by Jay E. Adams

Requests for information should be addressed to:
Zondervan, *Grand Rapids, Michigan 49530*

Library of Congress Cataloging-in-Publication Data

Adams, Jay Edward.
    How to help people change.

    (The Jay Adams library)
    ISBN 0-310-51181-X
  1. Pastoral counseling. 2. Counseling. 3. Change—Religious aspects—
Christianity. 4. Christian life—1960-   . I. Title. II. Series: Adams, Jay.
  Jay Adams library.
  BV4012.2.A3235 1986   253.5   86-12561

Printed in the United States of America

HB 06.07.2024

To Skip—
a faithful friend,
fellow counselor,
and fruitful workman
in the Word

Contents

Preface vii
Introduction xi

PART I: CHANGE, IN BIBLICAL PERSPECTIVE

1. The Need for Inner Change 3
2. The Four-Step Biblical Process 10
3. The Change-Producing Character of
   the Scriptures 20
4. The Sufficiency of the Scriptures 29
5. The Human and Divine Roles in Change 41

PART II: STEP ONE, TEACHING

6. The Importance of Teaching 51
7. Teaching God's Standards 58
8. Teaching Biblical Principles 72
9. Teaching in the Milieu 83
10. How to Teach 93

PART III: STEP TWO, CONVICTION

11. The Role of Conviction in Counseling 107
12. What Is Conviction? 111

13. Conviction and Data Gathering 119
14. The Use of the Scriptures in Conviction 125
15. Supplementary Thoughts About Conviction 132

PART IV: STEP THREE, CORRECTION

16. What Is Correction? 139
17. Correction and Repentance 142
18. Confession of Sin and Forgiveness 148
19. Forsaking Sin 153
20. Restoration 160

PART V: STEP FOUR, DISCIPLINED
          TRAINING IN RIGHTEOUSNESS

21. The Need for Disciplined Training
    in Righteousness 169
22. Righteousness: The Goal 174
23. But Is Righteousness Possible? 179
24. Biblical Training 190
25. Conclusion 201

Preface

The last 15 years have witnessed a profusion of well-meaning but ill-taught pastors and Christian workers attempting unsuccessfully to help others change. I get letters and phone calls from such workers all the time. When I go somewhere to speak, it is rare that people do not ask me for advice on how to help their friends and loved ones. Christians are buying books on counseling as if there were nothing else on the shelves. It seems as if the whole church has decided to do counseling.

It is encouraging that so many Christians are vitally interested in helping others. But try as they may, many run smack up against the hard realities, only to discover that their best intentions are no substitute for knowledge and skills. Though sincerely wanting to see change, they simply do not know how to bring it about. In order to help others, they first need help in understanding the counseling *process* itself. It is for such people that I have prepared this book as a guide to the process of effecting biblical change.

Cliff, a concerned Christian, has been counseling with Brad, a friend at work, who has confessed homosexual tendencies. Brad is not a Christian, and Cliff has plunged into the counseling without first confronting him with the gospel. As Cliff's efforts prove counterproductive, he wonders why he is unable to promote any real change. Cliff's ineffectiveness reflects a problem of order. He has gotten things out of sequence in the counseling process. Properly instructed about the process of counseling as laid out in Scripture, Cliff would have dealt with Brad much differently, beginning not with counseling, but with "precounseling" (i.e., evangelism).

Barbara has been served divorce papers by Phil, her husband of nine years. Both are professing Christians. Barbara doesn't want the divorce. But their church has never exercised church discipline, and, of course, she has never been instructed about what to do in such an event. The church has done nothing. Crushed and defeated, Barbara turns to her friend Mildred for advice and comfort. Although Mildred, a member of the same church, would like to help, she is equally untaught. So instead of pointing Barbara to Matthew 18:15ff., Mildred merely extends sympathy and tries to "comfort" Barbara by "talking it out." Her well-meant efforts soon turn into pity parties and later degenerate further into daily gossip sessions where both of their husbands are turned slowly on a spit, over fires fueled by resentment.

Whenever well-meant help is not biblically directed, it does more harm than good. It amounts to bad advice, leading to harmful action. Or else it leaves the situation unchanged by misdirecting energy, so as to produce more problems rather than solutions.

The upshot of Mildred's "counseling" is that it encourages bitterness and resentment, rather than cultivating conditions favorable to reconciliation. Without realizing it, Mildred has substituted a worldly process for the biblical one. Had she known God's process and how to use it, she would have proceeded very differently, probably with different results. The same could be said of Cliff and his counseling of Brad. Knowing and using the biblical process can make all the difference in the world: it can bring about change that honors God and helps others.

Some change comes swiftly, requiring minimal effort and little or no help from others. Other change comes hard and calls for the intervention of a counselor (Gal. 6:1). Since counselors are often stymied by the difficulties of bringing about the more stubborn sort of change, this book aims to set forth the scriptural ways and means of helping effect that kind of change.

Change of the easier sort often comes with simple biblical instruction, how-to guidance, and encouragement. Even such minimal assistance can be a problem to an erstwhile counselor who does not know the Scriptures well or how to implement them in particular situations. For such people, this book should afford more than ample information. But its focus is on the more difficult yet fairly common problems the average counselor encounters daily.

While touching on many aspects of counseling, this book does so from its own perspective. It is specifically designed to elucidate the process of counseling. I have often mentioned and illustrated that process, but not in the focused and systematic way that four-step biblical process is set forth here. Though ideas and procedures contained here may be found scattered throughout my other works, this book presents a fresh perspective not only on how to counsel, but also on what measures to take at what stages of counseling. It is a major effort to bring more ripened and mature thought to the counseling process, so that the average counselor will be able to use it in his day-to-day practice straight from the page.

Because this book readily could be used in a second or
third course in counseling, I have included assignments
at the conclusion of most chapters.[1] These, creatively
adapted, may be followed by instructors or by small groups
using this textbook. More assignments than are necessary
are given, allowing for choices and variety. Individuals,
reading on their own, also will gain more from the book by
doing the assignments.

May the God of all grace, Who has allowed me the
opportunity once more to write, bless these efforts to help
you help many others.

Jay E. Adams
Dean of the Institute of Pastoral Studies,
   The Christian Counseling and Educational Foundation
Director of Advanced Studies
Westminster Seminary in California

---

1. This book would be most useful in practical situations where the
student is already involved in regular counseling.

Introduction

Counselors agree on few things. Over the years I have stressed that the proliferation of counseling and psychotherapeutic systems strongly evidences both confusion and conflict within psychological and psychiatric ranks. The plain fact is that no consensus is possible on the prevailing assumption that man's problems can be solved apart from Jesus Christ. As most counselors scoff at the biblical views of man, God, and the universe, one should not be surprised at Carl Rogers's admission that the field of counseling is in a state of "chaos."

Given such disharmony, it might surprise you when I say that counselors of all stripes hold one point in common. No matter how divergent their dogmas, all counselors—Christians included—agree that the aim of counseling is to *change* people. Change—whether in the counselee's thinking, feeling, behavior, attitude, sensitivity, awareness, or understanding—is the goal of *all* counseling.

Because change is central to counseling and therefore vitally important, the Christian counselor must come to a scriptural understanding of change in all of its dimensions—its nature, goals, and process. Otherwise he might as well forget about helping others change, and when comparing ideas with counselors of a humanistic bent, he will have nothing better to offer. There is no excuse for being caught unprepared. In His Word, God has spoken definitively about change. But to become fully conversant with what He has said and to be able to organize and use biblical truth, it will be necessary for us to discuss both the process of change and its underlying theoretical principles. That we shall do in this book, but always with the focus on process.

Change versus Change

When we talk about changing people, what do we mean? Because counselors do not all have the same kind of change in mind, it is not strictly correct to say that they agree on the need for changing counselees. Just as the word *automobile* conveys strikingly different images to owners of new BMWs than to owners of third-hand Toyotas, so also counselors, who agree on the need for modification in counselees, may have vastly different ideas and attitudes concerning that change.

What we are talking about as Christians is change that goes far beyond minimal or incidental modifications in a person's behavior. The superficial change offered by secular counselors will not do. Substantial change requires the Holy Spirit's alteration of the heart (one's inner life known only to God and oneself). Outward changes of any significance must begin there. Anything less is an unbiblical and inadequate view of change.

"But must change be dramatic? Can't I genuinely help people change in small ways?" Yes, you can. Biblical change—for instance, the steady growth of believers—is not always one drama after another. Between the great spiritual strides are many small steps and seemingly minor changes, all of which are important because they flow from a heart transformed by God. Because a Christian's thinking, attitudes, and actions all pertain to his relationship to God, changes in any of those areas, whether large or small, are of central importance. That goes for changes both toward God and away from God. All counseling change is a matter of greater or lesser love toward Him. That is why the change that Christian counselors work toward is always crucial.

In other words, this book is not about neutral change. The change for which Christian counselors strive has a spiritual direction, and their aim is to help people prosper in that direction. All change toward God is good, and all change away from God is bad.[1] Sanctification, change toward God, is the goal of all Christian counseling. Successful counseling changes the Christian to make him more like Christ. Movement toward or away from the stature of Christ is a deeply moral issue, never neutral.

So, the change we are talking about is *substantial* change of a person's life. Brought about by the ministry of the Word, and blessed by the Spirit of God, it brings the counselee closer to the likeness of Christ. In short, it is significant change because it glorifies God.

Focus on Process

I have said that this book focuses on the *process* of helping people change. It is important to explain that word as well.

Although *process* is not a biblical word, the rest of this

---

1. Change affected by non-Christian counselors is not neutral either. In one way or another, it dishonors God, either by adopting attitudes or actions contrary to His will or by outwardly, hypocritically conforming to His law without a changed heart (a form of godliness that denies the power thereof).

volume will show that a definitive process of change is taught in the Bible. You don't get substantial change by throwing a switch. It requires carefully followed steps, specifically the four steps set forth in II Timothy 3:16. They form the process by which counselors may help people see progress in their lives.

The English word *process* is a compound term that weds the root ideas of "going" and "forward." As it is used today, it involves elements such as goals and objectives, movement and direction, ways and means, and order and steps. These add up to the idea of a series of interrelated steps designed to produce a certain outcome. The *Random House Dictionary* defines *process* as "a systematic series of actions directed to some end."

The process for effecting change in the life of a counselee, as described in the Scriptures, fits this general description. What makes the biblical process truly unique is the vertical dimension whereby substantial change takes place. Look again at the summary of change I have just given:

Substantial change

1. Is *"brought about by the ministry of the Word."* Note the gradual movement and ways and means. The ministry of the Word involves teaching, exhortation, rebuke, encouragement, discipline, etc., a series of steps.
2. *"Is blessed by the Spirit of God."* The Spirit is a unique factor in the process, not controlled by the counselor but essential to the process.
3. *"Brings the counselee closer to the likeness of Christ."* Thus you have direction and movement, along with goals and objectives.

There, along with the general elements of any process, is

the manifestly unique factor—the presence of the Holy Spirit and the necessity for His blessing in conforming the counselee to Christ, through God's Word. This vertical dimension makes all the difference, and yet, it is precisely this factor that so many counselors have missed. Because it has been so frequently ignored, that process is here placed on center stage.

Let us therefore take a hard look at the elements of a truly biblical counseling process and the place of the human counselor as he ministers the Word in the Spirit's power, to produce godly change.

Assignment

1. Compile a list of ten substantial changes required by God in the Bible that various counselees might be asked to make. Discuss ways in which these changes relate to God, have moral implications, move the counselee closer to God, and might affect the counselee's life.
2. Interview at least five pastors. Ask each to
   a. outline the process of change that he follows in counseling;
   b. discuss change and its place in his ministry.

Be prepared to discuss in class the strengths and the weaknesses of the counseling done by the pastors interviewed (name no names). The class should try to reach a tentative consensus from the total sample. The weaknesses will point to areas where special effort ought to be placed in this course.

PART I

CHANGE,
IN BIBLICAL PERSPECTIVE

1

The Need for Inner Change

When a marriage has become a boxing match, when a man has trouble keeping a job, when a person is so fearful that he will not leave his bedroom, or when a child tries to poison his parents, just about everyone agrees that change is necessary. I realize that R. D. Laing of Great Britain, and a few others like him, maintain that the so-called schizophrenics are not abnormal and that it is the rest of us who need to change (at least our evaluation of schizophrenia); but that rare and inconsequential view is the exception that proves the rule. When someone finds it difficult to get along with others, most agree that something's got to change, and therefore counseling is in order.

The Christian counselor agrees. But unlike his secular counterpart, the Christian considers a person's inability to get along with God to be an even more basic cause for counseling. Whatever one's other problems may be, there can be no change that is acceptable to God, and in the long run, to the counselee, until fundamental, positive change toward God has occurred. Most counselors, even many Christian counselors, overlook this crucial factor. Preoccupied with problems on the horizontal plane, they ignore or forget that problems must first be settled on the vertical. The two go together. The sum of the commandments is love toward God and toward one's neighbor. By linking those two great commands, Jesus made it clear that we must fully consider both dimensions. John, in his first letter, likewise demonstrated how you can't have the one without the other (I John 4:8; 5:1, 2). Biblical change must take fully into account both sets of obligations.

Taking seriously the vertical dimension makes it impossible to call the home-turned-into-boxing-arena purely a problem of immaturity or incompatibility or some other horizontal difficulty. If a couple persists in an improper relationship to God, they cannot long sustain a proper relationship to one another. Conversely, unresolved bad relationships with each other precludes good relationships with God. (See, e.g., I Peter 3:7: "Husbands, likewise live with your wives in an understanding way, showing respect for the woman as you would for a fragile vase, and as joint heirs of the grace of life, *so that your prayers may not be interrupted.*") Human relationships are a three-way, not a two-way affair. That means that biblically acceptable change takes into consideration one's relationships to both God and man. To that extent it is complex, unlike simplistic efforts to effect change without reference to God. Any counselor who wishes to counsel biblically must reckon with the complexities of change.

I do not wish to go into that matter very deeply here because I have treated it at length elsewhere.[1] But I cannot help noting how regrettable it is that many Christians have adopted simplistic counseling theories and practices, de-

---

1. See *Competent to Counsel* (1970), *The Christian Counselor's Manual* (1973), and *More Than Redemption* (1980).

vised by unbelievers, that have no place for God, let alone His centrality. When counselors eclectically accept these approaches, even their seemingly positive results go bad. Their best results are only *apparently* good. If God has been ignored in the counseling process, there is no way that apparently good results can hold up in the long run. Time will tell.

How is it that such results are only apparently good? If someone's fears are relieved, if a tottering marriage is stabilized, if one who could not hold a job learns how to do so, and if children stop poisoning parents, what is wrong with that? The question is fundamental and deserves a thorough answer.

In the eyes of the average Jew, the Pharisee was a good man. He kept the law, was a model citizen, and scrupulously observed the necessary religious rituals. By all appearances he was an upright man, whose life was in order and whose problems did not get out of hand. And, like the rich young ruler, who thought that he was good, the average Pharisee must have been fairly satisfied with himself. But Jesus saw it differently: "Unless your righteousness *exceeds* the righteousness of the scribes and the Pharisees, you will certainly not enter into the empire from the heavens" (Matt. 5:20). As He went on to point out, the righteousness of the scribe (religious teacher) and the Pharisee (a member of the strictest religious sect of the Jews) was all show and no substance, because it was not from the heart (see Matt. 6:1-5, 16-18; 15:1-20, etc.). It did not please God.

And yet this outward, socially esteemed religiosity, which followed the traditions of the elders, was deceptively satisfying to those who pursued it. We know this because Jesus represented the Pharisee as a self-sufficient, self-satisfied person in His parable of the Pharisee and the tax collector (Luke 18:9-14) and on another occasion declared, "Those who are healthy don't need a doctor; it is the sick who do" (Luke 5:31). The Pharisees would not repent of their sins precisely because they thought they were already good. In their own eyes, they weren't "sick" like "other people." They saw no need for the Great Physician!

What bearing has all this on change? Just this: outward change may appear good to others, even to oneself, *when in God's sight it is not*. If, for example, you stop robbing people, they still have their money, and you don't go to jail: the results are socially good. But, if that outward change does not involve a change of heart toward God, it creates a self-satisfied person who, to that extent, has become a Pharisee. External changes that do not follow an internal change of heart toward God always move a person further away from the Lord. So change that is socially good may be religiously evil.

"But isn't it good for people to stop robbing others?" Certainly, and the Christian should support laws that make it difficult to steal. But that differs from counseling designed to bring about change acceptable to God in the life of the robber.[2] Restraining evil is not the same as promoting good.

There are two kinds of competing "goods" in this world. Jesus had that in mind when He rebuked the rich young ruler, "Don't call any man good." Because he held a humanistic view of goodness, the young man thought he had become good by outwardly keeping the commandments, and he judged Jesus by the same standard. When, therefore, he called Jesus "good," he meant the opposite of what Jesus meant by that word. "Unless you are willing to call Me good *as God is good*," Jesus implied, "you must not call Me good at all." Jesus pressed the sharp distinction between

2. To attempt such change amounts to throwing "pearls to pigs" (Matt. 7:6).

the young man's apparent, outward, social, pharisaic, humanistic goodness and the goodness that flowed from His own sinless heart. So too, counselors must distinguish between righteous change, which comes from Christ, and the self-righteous change of modern-day scribes and Pharisees.

It is absolutely essential for the counselor to opt for change that is satisfactory to God, not merely socially good. Of course, it is better for people not to rob others—especially for the "others"! But when counseling, the Christian counselor is not making or enforcing laws. He is ministering God's Word to people's hearts. God did not call him to produce Pharisees, who conform no more than outwardly. The Christian counselor is to minister God's Word in a life-transforming way, such that God Himself changes the counselee—from the heart outward. The counselor's is a ministry not of reformation but of the gospel, which is always a ministry of transformation. The change that he seeks must be *substantial*, in which God brings the counselee closer to Himself.

Simplistic, superficial, and unsubstantial counseling teaches people to rely on self or on other men, while ignoring God. Counselees are led to think they "can get along just fine without the Holy Spirit, thank you." God has not called Christian counselors to manufacture more Pharisees; there are enough already. The more successful non-Christian counseling is in relieving the woes and the miseries of counselees and helping them fall in line with their culture, the more it produces Pharisees.

If I had to choose between putting a saloon or a liberal church on a corner, I'd choose the saloon every time. People who drink up the pay check in the saloon are less likely to become Pharisees, thinking that they don't need the Great Physician, than those who weekly swill the soporific doctrine of man's goodness. This is why "sinners" and "tax collectors" flocked to Jesus and the religious leaders did not. It was because He continually exposed the hollowness of their wicked lifestyle that these socially acceptable leaders ultimately put Him to death (see Matt. 23).

Many preachers would never dream of *preaching* change by reformation; they understand well that regeneration is essential to godly change. And they teach likewise that acceptable change in a regenerate person's life must come through the Spirit's sanctifying work from within. Yet, many of these same men come down from their pulpits and don an entirely different cap when they enter the counseling room. There they settle for a process of change that produces only outward, social results.

The obvious inconsistency between these two practices seems absurd until you recognize what has happened. These preachers have been sold a bill of goods at seminary, or in "Christian" books that promote eclectic counseling theories and processes. When marinated in religious language, this eclecticism often passes as Christian. But, again, its likeness to genuinely Christian counseling, in which the work of the Spirit is paramount, is only apparent. If anyone was religious, it was the Pharisee. Yet Jesus called for a righteousness that "exceeds" pharisaic righteousness, which is as filthy rags in God's sight.

The Pharisees, "out of ignorance of God's righteousness, and trying to contrive their own, didn't submit to God's righteousness" (Rom. 10:3). Counselees must not be led down the same path of unrighteousness by those who should know better. God has appointed Christian counselors as guides to a change that is directed toward godliness. Such change

  1.   Stems from an inward change of heart.

2. Is achieved by the Holy Spirit.
3. Is therefore entirely acceptable to God.

Nothing less will do.

As you can see, the process of change that must be followed by Christian counselors, by the very nature of things, will differ radically from all processes that address change on the horizontal level alone. It is substantial change because God Himself has brought it about. That is why we must study carefully what God has said about the process of change, become thoroughly acquainted with it, and be ready and willing at all times to pursue it in counseling.

Assignment

1. Exegete I Peter 3:7ᵃ, and, in a paper to be handed in, relate this part of the verse to biblical counseling.
2. From the writings of three Christians who use eclectic counseling systems, show how their principles and methods tend to produce pharisaism by ignoring the heart.
3. In the light of this chapter, study Proverbs 15:8, 9, 29; 21:4, 27; Romans 8:8. Be prepared to discuss these verses in class.

2

The Four-Step Biblical Process

In II Timothy 3:14-17, Paul wrote the following:

> You, however, must continue in those things that you
> learned and are convinced of, knowing from whom you
> learned them, and that from childhood you have known
> the sacred Scriptures, that are able to make you wise
> about salvation through faith in Christ Jesus. All Scrip-
> ture is breathed out by God and is useful for teaching,
> for conviction, for correction and for disciplined train-
> ing in righteousness in order to make the man of God
> adequate, and to equip him fully for every good task.

These words to Timothy contain a clear outline of the process all Christian counselors must follow if they would help
people change in ways that please God. These four verses
are so basic that this entire book is, in a sense, an extended
exposition of them. We shall therefore take the time to set
the passage in its context and to look in a preliminary way at
the steps Paul outlined as the biblical process.

The Context

Paul was writing his last letter. In it he told Timothy that

10

he was going to hand the torch to him. As his successor, Timothy would be expected to preserve God's good deposit (the gospel and related Christian truth), which Paul had taught him and, in turn, hand it on to others who would do the same (see chap. 2). Because Paul knew it would not be easy for Timothy, he took pains to alert him to the difficulties ahead. Many influences, tending to erode the truth, would be brought to bear upon the young man. Times would be hard; the period in which Timothy would take up his ministry would be marked by all that opposes the faith. To help Timothy recognize that period when it dawned and the evil forces against which he would be matched, Paul profiled that age in what we know as II Timothy 3:1-9.

In those "difficult times," as Paul called them, what would keep Timothy true? Paul himself would no longer be there to strengthen and encourage him. When all values would be tossed into the air, when the winds of moral degradation would blow with hurricane force, when the very fabric of human society would come apart at the seams, on what sturdy support could Timothy lean? What would help him to maintain his faith unaltered?

Paul pointed him to the Scriptures, and to the Scriptures alone: "Others may be influenced adversely by these strong pressures, but you, Timothy, need not be. If you cling to the Scriptures, you will remain true to the end. Your ministry will be useful, and you will find in them all that is necessary for you to carry it on successfully. So, focus your concerns on the Scriptures; they are adequate for every task to which God has called you in the ministry of changing men." That is the gist of Paul's message to Timothy and to every minister of the Word today who would remain faithful to God. Paul says that your efforts will be twisted and warped by the times in which you live, by the influences pressing in on all sides, unless you base your ministry *in its entirety* on the all-sufficient Scriptures (v. 17).

II Timothy 3:14-17

So much for the context. Let's now take an initial look at the passage before studying it in depth.

In verses 14-17, two thrusts clearly stand out, having to do with the two characteristics of Scripture:

1. The Scriptures are able (lit., "have the power") to make people wise about salvation.
2. The Scriptures are useful for teaching, for conviction, for correction and for disciplined training in righteousness.

Because these two uses of the Scriptures correspond to the two aspects of pastoral ministry, they are said to fully equip the man of God for his work.

The two uses of Scripture represent two stages in ministering to people:

1. People must first hear the gospel, believe, and be saved.
2. Believers must be built up in their faith by changing from sinful to righteous ways.

These two stages are evangelism and edification, and the Scriptures provide all that is necessary to carry out both.

Note the order: *first* comes evangelism; then, if that is successful, edification. As we have seen, trying to edify unevangelized people produces Pharisees. You cannot build where there is no foundation.[1] But the order of which

---

1. That was Cliff's problem when he tried to help Brad (see the Preface). See also the case continued in the note at the end of this chapter.

Paul wrote in II Timothy 3:15-17 shows the sufficiency of the Scriptures for carrying out Christian ministry in its totality.

The Four Steps

Within the process of edification itself are four steps:

1. Teaching
2. Conviction
3. Correction
4. Disciplined training in righteousness

Just as evangelism (and its goal, salvation) always must precede edification (and its goal, sanctification), these four steps must always occur in the same order.

That may seem like a bold claim. Can it be established that the four steps in the edification of the believer always take place in the order in which Paul has listed them? While Paul made no explicit statement to that effect, the very format of the passage strongly suggests it. First, Paul clearly presented the evangelistic and the edificational ministries of the pastor in what is universally acknowledged to be the only proper order: first evangelism, then edification. Clearly the idea of chronological order was in Paul's mind. That he would have indiscriminately listed under one of these ministries four elements, with no reference to order, just when he was thinking of order, is unlikely.

Moreover, when you try to imagine the four elements in some other order, you run into all sorts of trouble. That is just as unthinkable as reversing evangelism and edification. For instance, attempting the disciplined training of a counselee before teaching him what he must do, or before he is convicted that he should do it, or before he has corrected other erroneous and sinful ways, simply won't work. Moreover, there can be no conviction apart from teaching— one is convicted over against a standard. Similarly, correction is impossible for one who doesn't first know what is wrong.

While I am not prone to "discover" steps everywhere as some do (I don't even hold to steps in the Beatitudes),[2] it seems apparent that Paul had a definite order, or set of steps, in mind when he listed these four elements as factors in the edificational ministry of the church.[3]

The counselor's task is to promote change in the form of sanctification or edification. The four steps constitute the biblical process for doing so. In sanctification a regenerate person becomes more and more like Christ. This process is gradual, often irregular, and requires not only putting off old, sinful ways, but adopting new, righteous ones according to biblical standards.

In the passage Paul is saying that the four steps are not merely one process of change among many, but the only one the Scriptures set forth. The Scriptures, he says, will be found useful in your ministry to effect change in keeping with these four elements. And, he affirms, the process is sufficient to effect change that is pleasing to God.

The passage must not be limited to change brought about in counseling. Clearly, the entire ministry of the Word is under consideration. That ministry is twofold: public (preaching) and private (counseling), as Paul elsewhere asserts (Acts 20:20). While pastors must not lose sight of

2. Luke makes hunger the second and weeping the third, while Matthew inverts the order.
3. Calvin says, "Why begin with this word *doctrine*? Because it is the natural order" (*The Mystery of Godliness and Other Selected Sermons* [Grand Rapids: Wm. B. Eerdmans, 1950], p. 134).

that truth, in this book our attention is given to the counseling ministry alone.

Change in General

Let me make just a few general comments about change before moving on. As I have said, not all change is good.[4] Unlike Spencerian evolutionists, who seem to worship change because they believe (on blind faith!) that all change is progressive, Christians believe that any change not according to biblical standards is harmful. Christians say, "If the clock is too fast, set it back." No doubt the "difficult times" that Paul said lay ahead of Timothy were to be times of great change. But the change he foresaw was plainly bad. Only the Scriptures would keep Timothy and his converts from making the same wrong changes and would lead them, instead, into changes that would glorify God. Everyone changes constantly; the question is, in what direction?

Frequently change is not handled well. Studies show that many people become ill after times of significant change. That will not happen, however, if the changes are scriptural and are carried out in a scriptural manner. Wrong attitudes toward the change (i.e., resentment or fear), not the change itself, predispose a person to illness. Because we live in a world where nothing remains the same for long, it is important for Christians to learn how to handle change. The unbeliever has no assurance that behind the change is God, who providentially rules the universe. For many such persons who see through the foolishness of social evolution, change is capricious, meaningless, without purpose. Understanding God as the ultimate source of change is

4. The change described in II Tim. 3:1-13 represents change that is bad; it is change that is away from God, toward sin.

crucial to enabling the Christian to meet change without despair and defeat—the very attitudes that predispose one to illness. Indeed, some studies even indicate that cancer may be precipitated by such attitudes.[5]

As I have said in the previous chapter, the direction of all change is toward God or away from Him, and therefore change is moral. This factor must be uppermost in all considerations of change. There is no way to know what direction the change may have apart from a divinely given standard, the Scriptures. So we shall turn next to a consideration of what Paul had to say about the Scriptures in these verses.

Assignment

1. From other counseling textbooks, outline at least one other counseling process and compare and contrast the elements in that process with the biblical one.
2. Be prepared to comment in class on the uniqueness of the biblical counseling process.

Note

The following case, discussed in "Key to the Casebook," the *Journal of Pastoral Practice* 6, 1 (1982): 43, 44, illustrates well the importance of keeping evangelism and edification in their biblical sequence:

5. See Howard R. and Martha E. Lewis, *Psychosomatics* (New York: The Viking Press, 1972), p. 267.

KEY TO THE CASEBOOK
by Jay E. Adams

The Affair

(The Christian Counselor's Casebook,
Case No. 7, page 14)

Sharon and Eric, friends of one of your elders, at his suggestion have come for help in reconciling their marriage. They have been living apart for about one month, ever since Sharon found out about THE AFFAIR.

Eric declares: "She's frigid! What was I supposed to do?" as he openly tells of his subsequent unfaithfulness. There had been no sexual relations for over six months prior to his adultery.

"But don't forget to tell him about those times that you beat me . . . , and when you threatened my life! You were drunk, but I got scared! Billy (our son) won't even stay in the same room with you when you're like that. Everyone is afraid . . . and . . . fear and sex don't mix," Sharon cries.

"Eric, you are going to have to ask Sharon for forgiveness, and Sharon, you will have to forgive him if you expect to put this marriage together again," you counsel. "Moreover, we must discuss the even more basic matter of seeking God's forgiveness in Christ. That's where reconciliation and new life begin."

"I have forgiven him, but I can't forget. Forgiveness doesn't demand forgetting, does it? I know I love Eric, but I don't know whether I ever will be able to give myself to him again. You can't have good sexual relations when you are scared to death!"

This case delineates the all-too-common elements

that are found in many marriages today—charges and countercharges, blame-shifting, excuses, retaliation, etc. Perhaps the very first thing to notice is the number of problems itself. The counselor can't do everything at once; where will he begin?

Sharon's words seem to indicate a desire on her part to continue the marriage and to enter into counseling. With Eric, there is less of such evidence.

The counselor is correct in putting the emphasis where he does when he points to the need for pre-counseling (evangelism). Little else can be accomplished until Christ is in the center of the picture for all concerned. But he will go wrong if he expects Eric and Sharon to understand mutual forgiveness apart from first experiencing it from God. He must not allow Sharon to side-track him on a discussion of forgiving and forgetting at this point. He might say, "I'm glad you are interested in discussing forgiveness, because a Christian's forgiveness of another is modeled after God's forgiveness of him. So, let's begin by talking about forgiveness by God," thus bringing the discussion back to the major point.

The counselor will want to assure the couple that, in the Bible, God has answers to all of their problems, but that these answers are not available until they first are in the proper relationship with God Himself; these answers belong to His children.

There are questions about Eric: does he want to be present, or has he been pressured by the elder? Does he want to continue the marriage or not?

Presuming that both Sharon and Eric become Christians, subsequently the following matters along with others may have to be dealt with:

1. Using sex as a crowbar to pry what one wants out of another

2. Fear and love ("Perfect loved casts out fear.")
3. Drunkenness
4. Anger
5. What love is
6. Forgiveness and its obligations

While the sexual matter may have occasioned Eric's un-faithfulness (I Cor. 7:5b, he was not forced to respond to it that way. While fear of Eric may have chilled sex for Sharon, she could have overcome that with love (and, surely, for six months she didn't always have such fear). Sex was prob-ably being "used."

Many other observations might be made about this case, depending on how it progresses. But the principal factor to learn from it is to discover how to proceed, one step at a time toward clear objectives, not allowing steps that should come later to intrude at earlier points.

3

The Change-Producing Character of the Scriptures

Today the lines have been drawn between conservative, Bible-believing Christians and all others who purport to be Christians precisely on the grounds of their views of the Scriptures. Conservatives believe the Bible is the one inerrant, infallible rule of faith and practice; others do not. Everything rides on this point of contention: has God revealed Himself fully and infallibly in the Scriptures?

If you believe the Scriptures are the inerrant, full revelation of God's will to man, you will submit to them, whether you like what they tell you or not. If you believe in some lesser view of the Scriptures, you will bring them into submission to your reason, accepting what you wish and rejecting whatever does not please you. The minute you make yourself the judge of which parts of Scripture are authoritative and which are not, you slide into a morass of subjectivism from which there is no escape. As soon as you add another standard for belief or behavior, you take away from biblical authority. Here adding is subtracting, and the bottom line is no authority, no touchstone for life. That is why conservative Christians affirm that the Scriptures are inerrant, the sole rule of faith and practice.

Strangely enough, many of the most prominent de-
fenders of biblical inerrancy and authority are the very
pastors who, in counseling, treat the Scriptures as an insufficient source, in need of supplementation from psy-
chiatry and psychology. Sad to say, they implicitly deny the
Scriptures' credentials for helping people change.

What are those scriptural credentials? Paul presents five
of them:

1. The Bible provides all that a minister needs to carry
    on the work of the ministry.

That point is so critical to our study that we shall devote the
whole next chapter to it. Here we shall consider the other
four assertions:

2. The Bible is holy (or sacred).
3. The Bible is able (or powerful).
4. The Bible is inspired (or breathed out by God).
5. The Bible is profitable (or useful).

Each one of these assertions, made only in passing and
without elaboration by Paul, nevertheless tells us something significant about the Bible and its place in counseling.
Because of this we must take time to examine each in some
detail.

The Bible Is Holy

There are two words in the New Testament translated
"holy." The best known and most frequently occurring
word is *hagios*, which means "separated" and is the word
from which the terms *saint* and *sanctification* come. These
words speak of the Christian as one who has been "set
apart" from others to God as His *special* people. The other

term, used by Paul here in II Timothy 3:15 when he writes about the "holy" (sacred) Scriptures, is *hieros*.

The two terms ought probably to be distinguished in English by translating the first "holy" and the second "sacred." Admittedly, the ideas are close, and the difference is subtle. *Hieros* is used to speak of the temple (the *hieron*) as the "sacred place." It means, essentially, that which is consecrated to God, that which is peculiarly associated with Him. It speaks not of the character of the thing itself, but of its formal, external standing and relationship. That which is sacred is so because of its special, close attachment to God.

As paper and ink, the Bible has no inherent dignity. But because of its association with the message it contains and the One whose Book it is, it is sacred. It is a Book among books. Like no other book, it is closely associated with God Himself. It alone is His sacred (consecrated) Word.

The Bible, then, is unique; that is the point. You must not put it on the same level as other books. In it are things found nowhere else. In it is God's message, which has the power to bring men to faith in Christ and to bring believers into a closer relationship to God. It is truly unique because it alone is God's Book.

For that reason the counseling that flows from the Bible is unique. Far from being run-of-the-mill, it is unlike any other form of counseling. To put it simply, *it is sacred counseling*, and it follows *a sacred process of change*.

Such counseling and the change it produces have a unique relationship to God. He is their source. It is His counseling, and it is through this counseling process that He works by His Spirit. There is no promise that God will work through any other process. Why, then, should men—especially those who are orthodox in their profession of faith—add to (or ignore) the unique process of change set forth in God's sacred Book?

The Bible Is Able

When Paul wrote of the ability of the Scriptures to make a person wise about salvation in Christ Jesus, he literally said that the Scriptures "have the *power*" to make one wise. This same power to change human beings is what appears in the four steps of sanctification. God designed a biblical process to make a difference in those who heed it.

Just as the Holy Spirit "carried along" the Bible's writers (II Pet. 1:21) so that the writings of Moses or David or Paul were, at the same time, the Spirit's Word (see Heb. 3:7; 4:7; 10:15), so too *the Holy Spirit intended to change lives* through those Books. Every word of that perfect, inerrant Book is "from God" (*apo theou*), not from men, and was given for a purpose. As the Bible tells us:

> Whatever was written before was written for our instruction, that by the endurance and the encouragement that the Scriptures give us we may have hope (Rom. 15:4).

And,

> Now these events happened to them as examples and were recorded as counsel for us who live at this late date in history (I Cor. 10:11).

There is no useless material there. The Holy Spirit by the Scriptures brings men to faith in Christ and then molds them into the kind of people He wants them to be. The Bible is no mere history book; it *does* things to people *today*. It is the Holy Spirit's tool for working in the minds and hearts of men and women to make them like Christ. Being peculiarly associated with the Spirit both in its composition and in its use, the Bible is powerful, able to transform our lives.

Take for example the Gospel of John. The Spirit's purpose for moving John to write his Gospel is clearly stated: "These things are written that you may believe that Jesus is the Christ, God's Son, and that by believing you may have eternal life in His name" (John 20:31). Is it any surprise that verses like John 1:12; 3:16; 3:36; 14:1-6, and others have been used to bring more persons to Christ than perhaps any others? John's Gospel demonstrates its power to do what the Spirit designed it to do. So, too, all Scripture accomplishes its God-given purposes, one of which is to bring about righteous change in believers.

The Bible Is Inspired

Few words have been as misunderstood as the word *inspired*. It conjures up visions of someone sitting on a beach near Santa Barbara waxing poetic while watching the sun melt into the Pacific. We hear and read of "inspired writers," but that is not what the Bible is talking about. There were no inspired writers. They were—as I said, quoting Peter—"carried along" by the Holy Spirit, so that the final product was both theirs and His. But nowhere are the writers called "inspired." Indeed, much heretical thinking about the Scriptures has begun with the idea of inspired writers. The idea is totally unbiblical.

It is the Scriptures, the writings, not the writers, that God calls inspired. The books of the Old and the New Testaments are what the Holy Spirit inspired. There is a world of difference between inspired *writers* and inspired *writings*.

What does it mean to say that the Scriptures are inspired?

The language presents a problem, because the original Greek word actually says "expired," not "inspired." *Inspired* means breathed in; *expired* means breathed out. But although *expired* is the more precise term, it is hardly appropriate to Scripture, since librarians, not to speak of undertakers, have allocated it for purposes that are far afield. Then, too, the original Greek word is a compound term composed of the word for "expired" (or breathed out) and the word for "God." So in the light of all the confusion surrounding the word, it is perhaps best simply to translate literally, "All Scripture is *breathed out by God. . . .*"

Still, what does that mean? Let me tell you a story that should make it crystal clear. Some years ago I was in Brazil speaking to missionaries. One missionary, wishing to point out that Brazil is an illiterate country, asked me the following question: "If you had a secretary and you told her you were going to leave town for several days and that you wanted her to do so-and-so on Thursday, but before you left you thought better and wrote her a note telling her to do it on Wednesday, on which day do you think she would do it?" I answered, "On Wednesday, of course. She could always wave the paper in front of my face and say, 'See, this is what you wrote.' " "Exactly," he replied. "That is the way it would go in America. But not in Brazil. In Brazil she would always do it on Thursday. She would reason, 'I heard him say "Thursday" with his own mouth. So, he must have made a mistake when he wrote "Wednesday." ' " In an illiterate society the spoken word takes precedence over the written word.

Much of the ancient world was illiterate. That is one reason why the books of the New Testament were read to the congregations and why it is said that both the one who reads and the one who hears would be happy (Rev. 1:3).

Because an illiterate society might tend to undervalue the written Word, Paul assured believers, through Timothy, that "all Scripture is breathed out by God." That is to say, it is as much God's Word as if it were spoken audibly from His own mouth. If you were literally to hear God's voice, He would say nothing more, nothing less, and nothing different from what He has said in that Book. It is to be read, heard, and obeyed as fully as any literally breathed out words of God would be.

The process of change found in such a Book therefore is nothing less than God's own revealed process. God expects us to use this unique, powerful, and authoritative process in Christian counseling. Otherwise we had better not call it "Christian." Counseling, no less than preaching, is a ministry of the Word, dependent on the Scriptures for whatever it accomplishes. Just as there is no other authoritative source for preaching, so too there is no other authoritative source for counseling. There is no more room for the ideas of man in Christian counseling than there is in Christian preaching.[1] Counseling must be the ministry of the powerful, sacred Word of the living God Who, by His Spirit, works through it to change lives.

The Bible Is Profitable

Better than the King James translation, "profitable," is the ordinary English word, "useful." That is actually what

1. Indeed, if we could only get ministers to see counseling with Acts 20:20 vision as a ministry of the Word (its private personalized side) equal to the preaching ministry in importance, there would be little argument over whether eclecticism were possible. Bible-believing men refuse to be eclectic in preaching; similarly, they should refuse to be eclectic in the "house-to-house" ministry of counseling. See Calvin's Commentary on Acts 20:20 for some powerful words on the subject.

the apostle said. He made it clear that the Bible was given not for our amusement or to satisfy our intellectual curiosity, but for profitable use. To neglect that use is sin.

Unfortunately, some of the ways people use the Bible render it *useless*. When it is studied or taught merely for the sake of information, it becomes virtually trivial. Too frequently, even in conservative churches, people excel in Bible quizzes but do not know how to use the Bible on Thursday at work, in school, or at home.[2]

The Bible becomes worse than useless when it is put to purposes for which it was not designed. Since the Spirit had a purpose in every unit of material He caused to be written,[3] our task is to struggle with that passage until we know what He intended to do to us through it. For sake of ease, however, many use passages of Scripture for their own purposes. It is questionable whether the Spirit works in His Word when we handle it so carelessly. He Himself, through the apostle Paul, warned us that unless we do our best to become tried and true workmen in the Word, "handling the Word of truth *with accuracy*," we will have cause to be "ashamed" (II Tim. 2:15). The Spirit expects the Scriptures to be handled according to their intended purposes, not in other ways. Note, too, Peter's warning against "twisting" the Scriptures to one's own "destruction" (II Pet. 3:16). Twisting obviously refers to using the Scriptures in ways other than those intended.

So, using the Scriptures to learn doctrine for doctrine's sake and twisting the meaning of the Scriptures to suit one's

2. For more on this, see Jay E. Adams, *What to Do on Thursday* (Phillipsburg, N.J.; Presbyterian and Reformed Publishing Company, 1982).

3. For this reason, the *Reader's Digest* abbreviated "Bible" is a travesty. As John Murray said, ". . . no detail of what the mouth of God has spoken is dispensable" (*Selected Writings* [Edinburgh: Banner of Truth Trust, 1982], 3:262).

fancy are two dangerous activities to be avoided. God gave
us the Bible to transform lives. He gave it to evangelize and
to edify. To use it for other purposes is to misuse it.

The Bible is a practical Book. It embodies the commands
of Christ, which His church is *"to observe"* (keep and obey)
(Matt. 28:20). God's Word must be *ministered* to His people
in such a way that their lives are changed by it as they are
taught His standards for faith and life, are convicted of their
failure to live up to those standards, are shown how to
correct their sinful ways, and are led into new and righteous
ways in the future. That is ministry. It is just such a ministry
of His Word that God, by His Spirit, blesses. And that
blessing is demonstrated in the changed lives of His people.

Assignment

Write a major paper on "The Implications of Inspiration
and Authority for Christian Counseling."

4

The Sufficiency of the Scriptures

Inseparable from the four characteristics of Scripture we have just considered is its sufficiency. The Bible contains all that is necessary for a life of godliness. That axiom of the church's confessions was one of the Reformers' key points of departure from Rome. One would expect, therefore, that Bible-believing counselors, who already embrace such a doctrine, would for the same reason consider the Bible sufficient to bring about godly change in men. But things are not always as one would expect. Therefore, we must argue for the sufficiency of the Scriptures in counseling (from the Scriptures themselves, of course).[1]

In II Timothy 3:17, Paul wrote that Scripture was given

> in order to make the man of God adequate and to equip him fully for every good task.

Commenting on that verse, John Murray writes, "There is no situation in which we [as men of God] are placed, no demand that arises for which Scripture as the deposit of the

1. To argue on any other basis would be contradictory to the basic thesis.

manifold wisdom of God is not adequate and sufficient."[2] Three times and in three ways Paul emphasized the sufficiency of Scripture in this small verse, lest we miss the point:

1. The Scriptures make the counselor "adequate."
2. The Scriptures "equip him fully."
3. The Scriptures equip him "for every good task."

One wonders how Paul could have said it more clearly or forcefully! If they teach anything, Paul's words say that the Scriptures are sufficient for the work of counseling.

But just to be sure that we understand all that he was saying, let's look separately at each of the three statements about the Scriptures.

The Scriptures Are Adequate

What does the word translated "adequate" mean? The term is *artios*, meaning, "capable, fitted, complete, proficient"; or, as Arndt and Gingrich sum it up, "able to meet all demands." Paul meant that the Scriptures have the power to perfectly fit out the man of God for his task. He need never feel inadequate so long as he has the Bible. If he is inadequate, it is not because the Bible is inadequate but simply because he does not know his Bible adequately. The Bible has what he needs to meet all demands in counseling.

The Scriptures Fully Equip

Even more intensive is the second term, *exartizo*. This

2. Murray, *Collected Writings* (Edinburgh: Banner of Truth Trust, 1982), 3:261.

powerful and expressive word means to "thoroughly equip" for a task. In the papyri it is used of an oil press, completely furnished (see Moulton and Milligan). Also, before a ship was to sail, all contingencies on the journey would be considered, and supplies to meet each would be stowed on board (e.g., extra canvas from which to make new sails should the original sails be damaged); the ship would be "thoroughly rigged out." Mere men, of course, cannot foresee every possibility, and so their best plans often end in shipwreck. But God, the omniscient One, Who knows the end from the beginning, controls every contingency of history. When, therefore, He rigged out His "men of God" for their work, He neglected nothing. In the pages of Scripture are stowed every principle they might ever need to perform their tasks.

The Scriptures Equip for Every Good Task

True, the Scriptures do not contain everything. They are not a textbook for electrical engineering, shipbuilding (unless you are building an ark), aeronautics, or a hundred-and-one other disciplines. But they are entirely adequate as the textbook for living, and for changing our living to conform to God's requirements. Moreover, they teach nothing about unworthy tasks, but everything that the minister needs to know to perform his "good tasks."[3]

The words *pan ergon agathon*, "every good task," or "every good work," refer to the work of the "man of God" in bringing about the change described in verse 16b. The Scriptures supply him with all he needs to meet every

3. The word translated "good" is *agathos*, not *kalos*, which in a context like this might have been expected. The stress is on the moral character of his works, not on their beauty or perfection.

circumstance he might encounter in his work of ministering the Word. The Lord Jesus Christ, from the Old Testament alone, was able to handle every counseling case successfully. He was the world's only perfect Counselor, yet He had none of the "benefits" of modern counselors who now possess, in addition to the Scriptures, the writings of Freud, Rogers, and others! No, the church did not have to wait for over nineteen hundred years until Freud's day to perform its counseling task adequately. It had all it needed for that work from its inception—it had the Scriptures. That's what Paul said.

I must labor the point because many Bible-believing, Christian counselors eclectically maintain, contrary to all that verse 17 teaches, that something more is needed. That notion of "something more" must be abandoned, as counselors return to the Scriptures to discover all that God has stowed on board. Our problem is not that we do not have what we need in the Bible, but that we do not have enough of the Bible in us, which we need! If we study for a lifetime, we will still not exhaust this God-given Source of counseling principles and practice. The simple fact is that we don't have time to waste on weighty tomes written by benighted authors with clouded views of man's condition and needs, when so many brilliant shafts of biblical light have not yet illumined our counseling ministries.

There is no necessary relationship between Christian counseling and psychology. Let me explain that important and oft-misunderstood point in the remainder of this chapter by quoting an article that originally appeared in the *Journal of Pastoral Practice* 6, 1 (1982): 3-7.

INTEGRATION

by Jay E. Adams

It is strange how others misrepresent one's viewpoints. I suppose to some extent we are all guilty of doing so. And, I am sure that those of us who write soon come to recognize that no matter how carefully we try to guard against being misunderstood, there is nothing that can be done to prevent it. For instance, people are constantly saying that I believe all the problems that one faces are the result of his own sin. Yet, in my first book on counseling, *Competent to Counsel*, I clearly stated that this is not so, citing the cases of Job and the man born blind (John 9). Frequently since, in a number of my more than forty volumes, I have restated the fact from time to time in various ways—but to no avail; it seems people are still saying the same thing. Similarly, with reference to the subject that I shall address in this article, there is little or no understanding of my position and much misrepresentation. That is why, as in this case, it is important to take the time simply to clarify. While I know it will do little good for many, at least those who have the ears to hear and the eyes to read will know the facts.

The "in" counseling word in Christian circles today is integration. What is behind this word is the idea that the results of psychology may (many say must) be "integrated" with Christian counseling in some sort of fruitful union. The question, therefore, is asked in a dozen or more forms, "Do nouthetic counselors believe in integration?" In this article I shall attempt to give an adequate, though not exhaustive, reply to that question, the sort of reply that should serve to orient those who are concerned and provide direction for relating Scripture to psychology.

Fundamentally, I shall respond to the question with two answers:

1. There is no necessary relationship between psychology and Christian counseling.
2. There is a relationship between psythology and Christian counseling that can be fruitful.

Let me now try to explain those statements.

First, I have said "there is no *necessary* relationship between psychology and Christian counseling." The key word in that sentence is "necessary." By saying that any "integration" between the two must not be viewed as *necessary*, I mean that biblical counselors must not concede that Christian counseling is in any way *dependent* upon psychology for its existence or for the existence of any part of it. To assert that it is—as so many do, either by implication or by direct statement—is to run contrary to all of the biblical evidence (I have been presenting this evidence for years in books and will not replicate any of it here) and to invite all of the fundamental problems of eclecticism that I have been exposing for some time.

What I am saying on this point has been called "radical," "absurd," "simplistic" or described by any other number of pejorative adjectives. I agree that to the modern college- or university-trained Christian that is how it may seem. Even those who have studied in Christian colleges often suffer from the same myopic and insular sort of thinking that so often affects academes and their students rather than the more balanced view of theoretic practitioners (who are no longer enamored by and who have had opportunity to reflect on, go beyond and modify their own academic backgrounds). In academic circles eclecticism is the order of the day. That is because in these august halls there is a basic commitment to openness. This openness often consists of a willingness to hear as a viable option any or everything that may be presented.

But such openness will not do. God has revealed much truth in the Bible, and *we dare not open our thinking* (let alone our practice) to any theories or practices that prove to be out of accord with biblical teaching. Unfortunately, not too many persons—especially in the field of counseling—operate according to that presupposition. But, I insist, if we are to make headway in Christian thought in any area of life, we must agree not only that whatever God says in the Bible is true and authoritative, but also that because of this fact our minds must remain closed to anything that contradicts, attempts to supplant, or otherwise interferes with biblical principles and practices. If, operationally, Christian counselors would only adhere to this critical presupposition, they would save themselves much confusion and heartache and would realize more of God's blessing on their work.

Now, back to the word "necessary." When I say that there is no dependence of Christian counseling on psychology, I mean just that. Long before modern psychology was even a thought, Jesus Christ was the world's wonderful Counselor. In no way was His counseling dependent on the "findings" of psychology (ancient or modern). There was no *necessary* relationship between the two. All that He needed in order to counsel men and women perfectly about their problems was provided by the Old Testament Scriptures. The Spirit of counsel was upon Him to enable Him to understand and to implement the Spirit-inspired principles of the Word, but Jesus acquired the principles of counseling that He used to bring about godliness from the Scriptures alone. Christ never met a counselee that He could not help, and He never was at a loss to know what to say or do in any counseling context. From the Bible alone He gleaned all that was necessary to solve every counseling problem that He encountered. Nor was the church without resources for 1900 years—until Freud came. Paul makes it perfectly plain that all that was necessary for bringing about the process of change described in II Timothy 3:16 is fully provided by the Bible (cf. v. 17):

> All Scripture is breathed out by God and useful for teaching, for conviction, for correction and for disciplined training in righteousness, in order to make the man of God adequate, and fully to equip him for every good task (II Tim. 3:16, 17, *The Christian Counselor's New Testament*).

In verse 17 Paul says the same thing three different ways in order to make his point:

1. The Scriptures make the man of God adequate;
2. The Scriptures equip him fully;
3. The Scriptures enable him to perform every task.

These three descriptions of the power of the Scriptures to effect change in counseling all stress the Bible's sufficiency: nothing else is needed.

To postulate some *necessary* connection or dependency relationships between psychology and Christian counseling, affirming in one way or another that psychology provides *necessary* training, background, or even information for Christian counseling, therefore, is to

1. deny the Bible's claim to sufficiency;
2. deny Christ's adequacy as a Counselor;
3. believe that God left His church for over 1900 years without the necessary resources to solve human problems and live a godly life.

Because of all of these facts I must strongly dissent from any integrationist position that explicitly or implicitly maintains that Christian counseling is dependent *in any way* on psychology.

Is there a relationship between Christian counseling

and legitimate psychology then? Yes, of course. But let me make it clear what that relationship is and how it can be developed most fruitfully. I have said that the relationship is not a *necessary* one. Christianity has survived, and often survived well, without any such relationship for centuries. That means that the relationship must be occasional and *expediential*. Where it may be expedient to bring the two together, and according to biblical principles it is possible to do so, the Christian counselor may wish to make use of information garnered by legitimate psychological activities. As a relationship between business and psychology or music and psychology occasionally may be validly expedient at some points, so, similarly, will occasional relationships between psychology and Christian counseling fruitfully occur. But neither business nor music nor Christian counseling bears a *necessary, dependent* relationship to psychology.

Now, I have used the phrase "legitimate psychology"; surely you have noted the fact. By that phrase I intend to imply that some activities of psychologists are legitimate and some are illegitimate. Why do I make the distinction, and by what principle may the two be distinguished?

Both questions may be answered in one and the same response: Whatever purposes the Spirit of God says that He has provided the Scriptures to serve, it is illegitimate for psychology to attempt to redo. What God has done needs no improvement. I say this because (1) the Bible was given to the church for the pursuit of her work and not to psychology for its pursuits, (2) what God declares that He does His way it is not right for man to attempt to do in another way, and (3) if in the Bible God has already given us all that we need for counseling, it is unnecessary, if not impertinent, for man to supplement by (more to the point: to reject in favor of) his own ideas.

But what does the Spirit of God do through the Bible? As we have seen from II Timothy 3:16, 17, He not only supplies the data necessary for saving faith in Jesus Christ (cf. v. 15), but He also provides in that Book all that is necessary to bring about a process of change that will enable those who pursue it to please Him by walking in His ways. If a Christian perfectly followed what the Bible has to say (none do), he would solve all of his problems in such a way that no counseling would be necessary (except possibly counsel in biblical guidance).

The Bible hangs on two commandments: love God and love your neighbor (Matt.22:37-40). That is to say, the fundamental purpose or objective of the Scriptures is to enable a person to fulfil those two commandments. These two commandments are the subject matter of all counseling. Counseling has to do with the relationships of persons to persons (husbands to wives, children to parents, persons in business relationships to one another, friend to friend, Christian to an enemy, etc.), the proper relationship of which is love at all times and in every aspect of each relationship. Now, legitimate psychology does not cover that territory; illegitimate psychology, on the other hand, attempts to do so. When counselors speak of values, behavior, attitudes, and beliefs, as indeed they do, they transgress on the territory that God staked out for the Bible and its practitioners. Counselors cannot help but deal with such matters because they are dealing with the relationship of persons to persons (and, whether they know it or not, to *the* Person). Therefore, counseling is an illegitimate activity of psychologists. Anything else that a psychologist does, so long as it does not conflict with biblical principles or practices, is legitimate and from time to time may be brought into fruitful contact with Christian counseling—just as any other valid activity of life may be. But counseling principles and practices must stem from the Scriptures, not from some other source—the least of which is a source set up in competition to God to do precisely what God is in the business of doing. Substituting another, different and erroneous way (any way substituted for God's way will, by hypothesis, be erroneous), cannot be accepted.

But what of a truth that a clinical or counseling psychologist may have stumbled over—a truth that is not contradictory to the Scriptures? May we integrate that into our counseling theory and/or practice? After all, "all truth is God's truth."

If it is a truth that is *necessary* to counseling, it will be found already *in a purer form* in the Bible. There is no need to incorporate it as found—committed to a non-Christian system—into Christian counseling. What it may serve the function of doing is alerting the counselor to the need to study the matter to which it pertains more fully *in the Scriptures*. Usually, even when serving this useful function, on careful examination the principle or practice will be found to be only *similar to but not the same as* the biblical one. Care must be taken to distinguish things that differ.

"Well, if all of this is true, then what part may legitimate psychology play in Christian counseling?" A limited, but helpful one. Just as medical information about injurious practices (smoking, for instance) may fill out the biblical principle concerning the body and its care, so also may psychological studies regarding, let us say, sleep loss and its effects do the same. This "filling out" function, however, is not necessary to counseling, but it may be found useful.

It would be valuable for Christians in experimental psychology, and in other areas of psychology, who also view counseling as an illegitimate activity of psychologists, to unite with Christian counselors in exploring the areas where, occasionally, the two touch (1) to discover in what ways the two activities complement one another and (2) to develop ways and means for dialogue and cross-fertilization. Integration of *this* sort is not only possible, but desirable.

But, even here, one word of caution must be spoken: the Bible is absolute; the findings of any human discipline—including psychology—are not. Therefore, the authority of each differs, and our attitude toward "the latest results of psychology" must include an element of skepticism that, in contrast, we must totally remove from our study of the Bible.[4]

Assignment

Gather quotations from the writings of leading Christian counselors regarding the sufficiency of the Scriptures for counseling. What do they say? How well do their statements fit the systems they present? Examine their statements and their positions, using II Timothy 3:17 as a basis for your (no more than) five-page critique.

4. Of course, there is a difference between the Bible and our interpretations of it. But, because the same problem arises over psychologists' data and their interpretation of it, my basic distinction concerning authority holds.

5

The Human and Divine Roles in Change

Having looked at the Scriptures' credentials for producing change, especially the sufficiency of the Scriptures, we are ready to consider the roles of man and God in change.

Counselors risk shipwreck while attempting to sail safely between the shoals of two unbiblical extremes. On the one hand are the perils of self-help; on the other lie the dangers of quietism. The Christian counselor must avoid both. That means being aware of the unbiblical nature of these dangers and seeking always to follow the biblical course.

The problem is not so much one of balance as one of understanding biblical teaching and theology. Self-help advocates, in common with humanists, stress what man must do for himself. They are legalistic, moralistic, and, if biblically oriented at all, inclined to emphasize obedience to scriptural commands. Their assumption is that man can obey in his own strength. That is where the theological error arises.

On the other extreme of the continuum is an erroneous alternative to the self-help approaches: quietism. According to this view of self-abnegation, the counselee must

41

cease all attempts to do anything about his problems. Instead, he must make room for Christ to do what he has been attempting wrongly and unsuccessfully to do on his own. The slogan of such quietism is, "Let go and let God." Christ, or the Holy Spirit in the believer, is supposed to act *instead of* the believer himself. To the extent that the counselee attempts to obey God, therefore, he messes things up. It is Christ Who must do the obeying for him.[1] This construct likewise rests on a theological error.

Biblical theology teaches that both the counselee and Christ together must solve problems. As John Murray writes of sanctification in general,

> . . . the pilgrimage to perfection [in the eternal state] is not one of quiescence and inactivity. It is not "let go and let God." The journey proceeds apace with the most intense exercise on our part. . . . Our working is not suspended because God works, and God's working is not suspended because we work. The one is not superseded by the other. They are complementary. . . . Our working is grounded in God's working. Our working receives its urge, strength, incentive, and cause from God's working in us.[2]

Christian counseling is not an either-or but, rather, a both-and process that involves the Holy Spirit and the believer. They work together to solve problems God's way, according to God's Word. To expect the counselee to obey in his own wisdom or strength is unbiblical. But in the light of all

1. The utter fallacy of the position is that, logically, the sinner should say, "When the Lord enables me to, then and only then will I try to stop my adulterous habits. I dare not try to do so myself." Even quietists fall short of such an absurdity.
2. Murray, *Collected Writings* (Edinburgh: Banner of Truth Trust, 1982), 3:266, 267.

of the biblical commands given to him, it is equally unbiblical for the counselee to do nothing while waiting for God to do everything. There is a proper role for both the human and the divine in biblical counseling. Those who are true to biblical theology understand this interrelationship and refuse to create unbiblical dichotomies where God Himself has done just the opposite.

The human role in effecting change is seen in both the abundance and nature of the biblical directives God calls upon the counselee to obey. Self-help people correctly see the *necessity* for obedience, but are wrong to imagine that the counselees in themselves are capable of obeying. That is where the quietists have a point: the Holy Spirit alone supplies the power and wisdom for such obedience.

The human role in counseling is evidenced in the responsibilities of the counselor as well. Human counselors participate in the process as they minister the Word to counselees, instructing, encouraging, and helping them to implement biblical injunctions. While, like counselees, they may try to usurp the place and work of the Holy Spirit, that is not a necessary consequence of their efforts. We know this because the Spirit Himself gave pastors and teachers to the church to counsel and guide the flock.

Scripture makes the divine role in counseling equally clear. The Holy Spirit produced the Book from which all of the precepts and the examples must be drawn in reaching God's solutions. And the Holy Spirit alone convicts and changes the counselee as He enables him to understand and obey the Book. It would be impossible for the counselee to follow biblical mandates apart from His enabling, strengthening, and enlightening power. Nor could the counselor understand or properly minister biblical truth with wisdom apart from a similar work of the Holy Spirit within him.

As you can see, four elements emerge in the process of counseling, which must be interrelated: the Spirit, the counselor, the counselee, and the Bible. It is important for us to look at how these participate in the interaction between the human and the divine.

The Spirit and the Book

The Bible itself is a prime example of human and divine interplay. It was composed both by the individual human authors in their various styles and vocabularies, and by the Holy Spirit, Who motivated them to write, arranged the circumstances, guided the formation of their styles and vocabularies, and superintended their writing so as to produce an inerrant book. Much error about the Bible, as well as about Christian counseling, stems from neglecting either the divine or the human aspect. We must do neither.

When the Spirit produced the Bible through divinely aided human means, He produced it for a purpose. It was not to be ignored, but was to be understood (through His enlightenment) and obeyed (through His power). The Bible's many commands—directed to both counselees and their counselors—are to be obeyed. The Spirit did not intend to ignore the Book or for us to do so; rather, He intended to *use* it for the purposes for which He caused it to be written, chief among which is to change the lives of His people.

That the Holy Spirit operates through the Bible is also confirmed in that what the Bible is said to do, the Spirit is likewise said to do. For example, each of the four functions of Scripture (listed below) is said to be performed also by the Holy Spirit (in the verses added):

1. "Teaching": compare I John 2:27 (The "anointing" represents the Holy Spirit.).
2. "Conviction": compare John 16:7-11.
3. "Correction": compare Galatians 6:1; 5:22, 23.
4. "Disciplined training in righteousness": compare Galatians 5:16-18; Romans 6–8.

In each case the Spirit works *by means of* the Bible. Contrary to much that is taught today, the counselor must affirm that the Spirit does not work outside of the Bible, but through it. He should accept no mysticism; there is no biblical warrant for it.[3]

Direct revelation or promptings and checks from the Spirit (as though He operates today through some internal Urim and Thummim) must be neither sought nor expected. Some, thinking that the Spirit's will may be discerned from feelings or other indications external to the Scriptures, have wandered far from biblical principles. Good counselors will neither allow counselees to do that nor be guilty of it themselves. The Bible offers not the slightest encouragement to follow extrabiblical hunches (no matter how "spiritual" they may seem) or other substitutes for biblical exegesis and application. It is dangerous to depart from the Book by which alone the Spirit has promised to effect the changes we need to make.

---

3. Two days ago, a man purporting to do Christian counseling told me that when he counsels a woman who has aborted her child, he has her ask the Spirit for the sex of the child. On the basis of this information, he tells her to name the baby and seek its forgiveness. Such nonbiblical procedures stem from an attempt to contact the Spirit directly, as one seeks direct information from Him, not mediated through Scripture. In this case it led to praying to the dead and possibly spiritism!

The Counselor and the Book

Another relationship we may note is the relationship of the counselor to the Bible. Because, in effect, the entire book is dedicated to exploring this subject, my comments here will be brief. They could be summed up by saying, "If the Bible is good enough for the Spirit, surely it ought to be good enough for the counselor!"

Just as the biblical counselor discovers the closest relationship between the work of the Spirit and the words of His Book, so too should he endeavor to work in the closest harmony with the Bible. That is how he works with the Spirit. The counselor must neither add to nor subtract from God's Word, but offer those needing help "the whole counsel of God," which Paul declared "beneficial" to the church (Acts 20:20, 27). Rather than seek help outside of the Scriptures, the Christian counselor has the privilege and the obligation to search the Scriptures continually until he learns the mind of the Spirit. His search must be prayerful, and his study must be scholarly, accurate, and full of devotion. He must ask the Spirit, Whose Word he is endeavoring to understand and apply, to enable him to do both. But he must not expect the interpretation to come magically, without effort on his part.[4] In other words, like the counselee, the counselor has a job to do, in understanding and acting upon the Bible, acknowledging always that the Counselor behind all his counseling is the Spirit Himself.

4. The Greek word *spoudazo* (II Tim. 2:15) translated "study" in the KJV and "do your best" in CCNT, means "to give diligence." It involves the idea of activity, in some contexts even carrying the meaning "to make haste." Surely *biblical* counseling calls for zealous, diligent effort. Understanding of the Scriptures is not obtained by mystical means but by diligent study; successful ministry of the Word does not happen magically but by zealous, careful use of the Scriptures.

The Counselor and the Counselee

Again, the human and the divine must be paramount in our thinking. Human counselors addressing human problems tend to adopt humanistic approaches. But II Timothy 3:16, 17 speaks of a counselor who does not counsel in his own wisdom or strength: he is called a "man of God." That phrase, which Paul drew from the Old Testament, is used in the pastoral epistles for the minister of the Word. It speaks of him as a *representative* of God. While he is human and will always acknowledge that fact, the counselor does not minister in his own name. He ministers as one who represents God, as one who speaks for Him, as one who knows the mind of the Spirit and who will minister out of the Book in which that mind is found. He cheats the counselee when he does anything less. And he misrepresents God whenever he doles out an admixture of human error and divine truth.[5] The man of (from) God is to be heard inasmuch as he bears authority from God.

While a counselee may appeal a judgment of a biblical counselor, he should do so only on the basis of the Scriptures. Counselors may be wrong, but they are to be heard, and they are to be obeyed when they make their case from Scripture rightly interpreted and applied (see Heb. 13:17).

An important difference must be noted. Whenever a counselor commands a counselee from a clear passage of

5. Note that according to I Kings 17:24 a "man of God" is one who has God's Word in his mouth. It is distressing when the mouths of those who were called to be men from God, representing Him and bearing His messages, are filled with men's wisdom instead (or, in Rogerian fashion, are empty, with no Word from God). Timothy is rightly called a man of God because he not only knew the Scriptures but followed the Word of God given through the apostles, which is now recorded as the New Testament (II Tim. 3:14, 15a).

Scripture ("You must stop committing adultery"), he commands with all the authority of God Himself. But when he implements the command with his own suggestions as to how it ought to be obeyed ("I suggest that you phone the woman right now and tell her that you are calling it off"), he has no such authority to command. That is why in the example in the last parenthesis I represented him as saying, "I suggest." The how-to is not always spelled out in the Bible. And there may be good reason for fulfilling the same command in a different way. Counselors must not confuse biblically *directed* how-to with biblically *derived* how-to. To treat the latter with the same authority as the former is to become an authoritarian rather than a biblical authority. In the long run, it will minimize the counselor's true authority as well.

It is important to recognize in these relationships the biblical balance for ministry in which the human and the divine each play a part. That balance may be achieved only by correct theological thinking. The power, the wisdom, the strength are all from the Spirit, but the action is to be taken by the counselor and the counselee.

Assignment

Study carefully the following Scripture passages and from your study be ready to discuss further the relationship of the human to the divine in the ministry of the Word. If desired, different groups could be assigned particular passages upon which to report. I Thessalonians 3:2; Hebrews 13:21 (cf. I Peter 5:10; 4:11); Philippians 4:19; Ephesians 3:16; Colossians 1:11, 29; I Corinthians 3:6; Romans 1:11, 12; Ephesians 4:16, 17, 20; I Timothy 1:12; John 15:5b; I Peter 4:11; II Peter 1:3; II Corinthians 3:5; Luke 21:36; Philippians 2:12, 13; Romans 12:2; 5:5; II Timothy 2:1.

PART II

STEP ONE,
TEACHING

6

The Importance of Teaching

We come now to the heart of this book: a detailed consideration of the four steps of the process of change, in the order set forth by Paul. The first step is teaching.

We have been living in an irrational era. A wave of irrationalism, heralded by the advent of existentialism, Freudian irresponsibility, and the general disillusionment brought about by two world wars, has drenched the West. We have endured the drug culture, nihilistic abstraction in art and music, love of violence, the overthrowing of all restraints in sex, occultism, and an influx of Eastern religions. Interest in something as rational as teaching has waned.

When the pendulum completes its long arc into irrationalism—which appears will soon occur—it will once again head back toward rationalistic thought.[1] Teaching and all of the cerebral activities connected with it will once again reign supreme. In their concern for teaching in counseling, Chris-

1. That is, toward Greek intellectualism, according to which "knowledge is virtue" and "no man does evil voluntarily."

tians must not be caught up by the swinging pendulum as they so often have been in the past.

During the craze over spiritism and the occult, for instance, there was a parallel interest in demonism on the part of Christians; the swing of the pendulum swept large segments of the church with it.[2] Likewise, as Christian eclectic counselors have been carried along with the times, they have adopted the views and methods of feeling-oriented counseling systems. They have brought into the church the love-yourself, self-worth, self-image ideas of Maslow and others. And in the years ahead, the temptation will be to adopt the rationalistic systems of men like Albert Ellis and others yet to appear on the scene. That temptation must be resisted.

The Christian does not need to oscillate with the times (though he must understand and come to grips with them). With the Bible to keep him in balance, he need follow neither the rationalist nor the irrationalist. His motive for teaching is not the latest trend but the biblical imperative. Though others have been saying, "follow the feeling," and "just listen; don't give advice," that has not dissuaded nouthetic counselors from teaching counselees. In the same way, if Ellis and others begin to discover the importance of teaching, we will not stop teaching just to be different. The teaching imperative stands, because it is a part of the sacred process of change that God Himself sets forth in the Bible.

Whatever teaching others may do, ours will be distinct both in content and in form. The content will be biblical, not, for instance, the rational-emotive doctrines that Ellis borrowed from Epictetus, Marcus Aurelius, and other Stoics. And the form will be teaching by discipline. A supracultural method, discipling has its roots in the relation-

2. And many unbiblical teachings and practices were followed.

ship of the Trinity (in ways, of course, that we cannot understand). In John's Gospel, where Jesus describes His ministry (chaps. 3, 5, 8), He makes it clear that His teaching consists of what He has seen the Father do and heard the Father say. Learning by hearing and seeing—that is discipling. In the midst of such discussions, Jesus tells us that if we will do what we have seen Him do and say what we have heard Him say, we too will be His disciples. Thus, we must take our cues from this biblical method of teaching and understand that when we teach what the Bible teaches, we too must use the show-and-tell method.

Discipling assumes that we are willing to adopt the scriptural, whole-person approach to counseling. We become not only biblical authorities who tell counselees what God says they must do, but also persons who do those things ourselves. That means being willing to share from our own experience and exemplifying what we are saying, as well as pointing to other models of Christian thinking and living in the counselee's daily experience from whom he may learn. We will teach, but we will always "teach to *observe*" (Matt. 28:20). In no other way can we "make disciples" as we are commanded. Our teaching must be of the sort that the Lord commanded. And it calls for great care, because, as He once said, "When he is fully trained, the disciple will be like his teacher" (Luke 6:40). Please note, Jesus did not merely say "think" like his teacher, but "be" like his teacher. Holistic teaching takes place whether we know it or not, whether we like it or not. We cannot avoid it. That is why it is important to be sure that we know what is being taught by our lives, as well as our lips. Any dichotomy between the two is false and unbiblical.

As for the content of teaching in counseling, you may need to teach any or a combination of those commands to which Christ referred in Matthew 28:20. A counselor must never become a least-common-denominator theologian and exegete. He must become familiar with the entire corpus of Christian doctrine and continually grow in his understanding and application of it to life.

"The whole corpus of teaching in the Scriptures? Why so much?" Simply because every truth in the Scriptures has implications for living. There is no doctrine given for merely abstract reasons. Even the great teachings about the deity and the humiliation of Christ found in Philippians 2 were given in a practical context and for practical purposes. Paul's bold use of profound teaching for practical purposes is instructive, and we must learn from it. Every element in the "whole counsel of God" is useful for counseling.[3]

Because even profound doctrine is important to counseling cases, a Christian may never beg off, saying, "Well, my Sunday school training will suit me just fine for counseling." Few openly do that, but from the shockingly superficial understanding and misuse of the Scriptures among even some of the best-known Christian counselors, one wonders how much biblical and theological training they have had and how much effort they expend in trying to interpret and apply the Scriptures accurately. Their grasp on the writings of the psychologists and the psychiatrists seems much tighter, sad to say. If, however, you wish to be a faithful minister of the Word, you will be constantly "into" the Scriptures, untying knots in your thinking, coming to correct interpretations of passages, thinking through the implications of doctrine (I Tim. 4:15). You will do all you can (with the help of the Holy Spirit) to become a

---

3. For help in these matters and in much that follows, see my book, *More Than Redemption*.

workman in the Word who doesn't need to be "ashamed" because he has been "accurately handling the Word of truth" (II Tim. 2:15). It is a fearful thing for a "man of God," whose role is to represent Him, instead to misrepresent Him.[4] Not only is God Himself dishonored as we tell lies about what He says, but the counselee is led astray and harmed. Whether intentional or not, these lies misrepresent what God has said and lead His children into the wrong paths.

It is, therefore, a fearful thing to be a biblical counselor, and we must recognize the fact. We are not Rogerians who never teach anything; we are men from God who must speak and live His Word. And just because we are that, we must remember that "we teachers will receive stricter judgment" (James 3:1b). There are many persons calling themselves Christian counselors who should give much more thought than they apparently have to what God has said about this responsibility.

So, the first thing we must understand is that the entire Bible is important in counseling; we can neglect no part. That means that in the process of counseling the biblical counselor may be called upon by the counselee and his circumstances to range far and wide over biblical territory he does not travel every day. He must know the way. He cannot familiarize himself with a list of fifty or even a hundred verses, half understood, and let it go at that.[5]

4. But speaking erroneously cannot be avoided by adopting a Rogerian-like posture in counseling. Not to speak is as wrong for a "man of God" (one who represents God and from whose mouth, we have seen, God's Word must be heard) as to speak error. God is misrepresented by Christian counselors when, adopting Rogerianism, they give the impression to counselees that God has nothing to say about their problems.

5. Recently a Christian who purports to do biblical counseling told me

For example, he must master all of the intricacies of the biblical issues concerning marriage, divorce, and remarriage. Otherwise he will wreck lives by giving poor advice, as so many have. He must be able to articulate the biblical teaching about church discipline, show what the Bible commands, and know how to implement it in actual cases. He must know how to handle questions of conscience, with a thorough understanding of the holding principle in Romans 14:23b, as well as how to grapple with a counselee whose conscience has been misinformed, or seared with a hot iron. He must be able to work his way through all of the aspects of sin, guilt, confession, and forgiveness with surefootedness. He must be able to sort out biblical warnings and promises and know how and when to use each. In short, he must have solid, biblical reasons for every piece of advice he dispenses. After all, he is to be a "man of God," not a "man of men." He must not use the Bible to "support" the ideas of counselors whose views bear only a vague resemblance to biblical truth. No, he must be sure that what he does is truly in accord with the Scriptures. It is his task to *teach God's Word*, the Bible, not the ideas of men (even if they are his own).

Naturally, he will not learn all of these things at once. But unless he works constantly on these and dozens of other issues like them, he is not fit to be called a *Christian* counselor. Let him set himself up as a counselor, if he will, but let him drop the adjective.

If a counselor must teach God's Word that way, he must

that he is able to do so with the use of just a half-dozen verses! If anything less than the "whole counsel of God," which Paul declared "beneficial" (Acts 20:20, 27) is adequate, then God surely erred in providing such a large and comprehensive Bible. Paul says that "all" Scripture is "inspired" and *"useful."*

know what he is doing. Therefore, we shall take the time to delve into some aspects of.teaching that are necessary in counseling in the chapters that follow.

Assignment

Study teaching by discipling in the Scriptures. Be prepared to discuss in class at least five distinct ways in which a counselor might disciple a counselee.

7

Teaching God's Standards

Ask any four Skinnerians, "Is it true that you can make any kind of sausage you want?" and the answer will come back, "Yes, we can." Skinnerians agree that out of the other end of their "meat grinder," the behavioristic process, they can produce any sort of person a human being is physiologically capable of becoming. Given the proper contingencies plus an adequate reward and "aversive control schedule" (their euphemism for "schedule of punishment"), they can train the human animal (and for Skinnerians that's all man is) to do whatever they wish.

"I see," you say, "but now, tell me what kind of sausage should we grind?" One answers, "Polish sausage." Another counters, "No, I think Italian sausage would be better." The third insists, "Give me celery sage every time." And the fourth meekly chimes in, "It doesn't matter to me; I like them all."

Do you see the problem? Granted, for the sake of the argument only, that the Skinnerians have the "sausage grinder" (they don't), and that they can turn a human being into virtually any kind of person possible (they can't). You

58

could never get them to agree on what that human being should look like. Pressed hard enough, their ideas of the ideal human being would differ according to each man's likes and dislikes, code of ethics, and whims. They would not agree on what kind of sausage to produce.

That is the fundamental problem of all counseling systems: counselors are out to change others, but they can't agree on what the end product should be like. The fundamental question is, "Change people—into what?" It is a question of standards.

Skinnerians lack adequate standards. But they are not alone. (I mention them only because they claim to possess a sausage grinder.) Many systems fail to come to grips with the fundamental question they all must face: "Change people? Into what?" Effective counseling *moves people* from one point to another. "To what point should one travel; what is his proper destination?" That is the question.

Because one man's opinion is no better than the next, it is sheer arrogance to tell a counselee, "You must adopt my standards." Regardless of what is said or done, counseling without a Bible represents arrogance. If a non-Christian counselor says, "I know what is best for you," there it is—arrogance out in the open. If he says, "We'll adopt Freud's or Ellis's or Laing's standards," there it is again, but not quite so far out front. Still it is *he* who has determined whose standards are to be adopted. Even if he says to the counselee, "I won't set goals for you; you must set your own," there it is once more, still further back, but there. He is saying in effect, "*I* know that the best thing for a counselee is to allow him to set his own goals." No matter how you squeeze it, ultimately it is *he* who determines what standards are acceptable—even when they come from a human source other than himself.

In contrast to all of this, Christians are committed to standards that are not human but divine. "Wait a minute," you protest; "how have you escaped the problem you pointed out in the previous paragraph? All you've done is hide the fact that *you* accept God's standards as correct. You are no better off than the rest."

I know it seems that way, but you are quite wrong. There is a difference. I have no choice in the matter. I have been ordered by God to accept His standards, ordered in a way that no human being has a right to order me. Secondly, my standards are unaffected by sin; they come directly from the hand of the sinless Son of God. Thirdly, I would never have accepted these standards on my own. As an unconverted sinner, I considered them repugnant (see I Cor. 2:14). Only as I have been transformed by the Holy Spirit am I willing (if not always anxious) to accept them. So there is a great difference. "But," you continue, "all that presupposes that these things are true." Of course! That is my presupposition.

If what I have said sounds like a circular argument, that is because it is. In the long run, there is no other way to argue, no matter what position you take. You must reason, if you reason consistently, from your basic presuppositions, which you accept by faith. We are all committed persons, whether we know it or not. I am committed to Christ, and the Scriptures as His Word, my standard for faith and practice. I could argue in no other way; to do so would be to deny my salvation and my Lord.

Because God exists and has given us real standards, we can know for sure what a person should look like. We can know the proper goals for counseling and the answer to the question, "Change a person—into what?" Giving a firm and certain answer is by no means arrogant when the standard to which we call counselees is the same standard to which God has called *us*. We too must submit to it by faith. The call we extend to others is but an echo of His call to us.

Counselors ought to have grave doubts about the worth of manmade standards, given their abysmal record. And what's more, with so many competing value systems abroad, to accept any with assurance requires either raw gullibility or unabashed arrogance.

Just what should a person look like? If you are a Christian, you know the answer. A counselee should look like Jesus Christ; He is the standard. The Bible, by both precept and example, gives us a complete record of what Christ is like. Read the Ten Commandments; Christ fulfilled them perfectly, as the accounts of his life show in detail. Read about the fruit of the Spirit; again, His life and ministry are an active portrayal of love, joy, peace . . . in perfect profusion. Christian counselors have a standard on which they can agree with each other, as well as with their counselees.

The Bible is the standard not only for what the counselee must become, but also for how he must become it. Both his target lifestyle and all that goes on in counseling toward that end must measure up to God's Word. Biblical ends in counseling must be attained by biblical means.

Standards That Stand True

The principles of change given in the Bible are transcultural. With minor adaptations they can be translated into the lives of people on any continent and in any sort of culture.[1] The Book of Acts demonstrates this fact. Biblical

1. In such adaptation the *counselor* must be flexible, not the standard. Christian counselors are servants, not stodgy, self-sufficient profession-

standards have, indeed, made and remade cultures (e.g., what the Bible has done to transform the West since the Reformation[2]). The basic problems of human beings in the Orient, in Africa, in Europe, or "down under" are the same. All must learn to love God and one another. The Bible addresses man's fundamental problems—having to do with sin, salvation, and sanctification—whatever form those problems may take culturally.

Moreover, the Bible's standards do not fluctuate. How difficult it must be for the non-biblical counselor to determine when to shift his standards (perhaps following the lead of a fickle society or the American Psychiatric Association). When the American Psychiatric Association, under pressure from homosexuals, determines by vote that homosexuality is no longer to be considered abnormal, that must make the average counselor wonder about lasting values. As when the pope decreed that eating meat on Friday was suddenly all right, or when the Mormons admitted Blacks to office, though for years they were considered a cursed race, fluctuating standards among counselors must cause a great deal of anguish in those who try to make sense of them.

The Christian has no such problem; he has a set of abso-

als. The height of professionalism is seen when the counselee is required to adapt to the professional, usually for the latter's convenience. Servanthood is seen in adapting to the counselee (see I Cor. 9:22, where Paul says, "I have become all sorts of things to all sorts of people." He does not say, "My *message* has become all sorts of things.

2. The Bible isn't a Western book; yet it has become the standard for Western culture, sharply contradicting all culturally bound viewpoints. Indeed, more often than some advocates of extreme contextualization seem to think, the culture should be molded by the faith (where it is out of accord with the faith). Cultures are tied to beliefs and practices and will tend to pull one back into those beliefs and practices unless both are consciously altered.

lute standards, which pertain to man in all generations. He does not have to apologetically abandon yesterday's practices when the rest of society does. God's standards don't become obsolete: let all men be liars and God be true! The Christian may not always find it easy to maintain God's standards in the face of many pressures to back down. But those pressures seem minimal when compared with the agonizing problem of wondering whether your standards will withstand time or scrutiny.

Since no Christian totally understands the Scriptures, the believer must from time to time adjust his standards, as his understanding grows. But what a difference to know that what you have truly learned is firm and unchangeable and that even the changes you make are not in the standards but simply in your comprehension of them. Although the unbelieving counselor cannot say with assurance, "You must not commit adultery," the Christian can. That standard is simple, straightforward, and firm, as are scores of others. Therefore the Christian can counsel with a certainty and an assurance unattainable by others. For example, he can *know* that drunkenness and homosexuality are forgivable sins, not diseases or genetic defects. And he can *know* that the threats and the promises set forth in God's standards will come true. To have that sort of certainty makes a great difference in how one counsels.

Such certainty lends an authority to one's counseling that others cannot have. It enables the Christian counselor, as a "man of God," to make promises in God's Name, according to God's Word. He can therefore encourage a hope in the counselee when others cannot. The hope he offers is sure, based on the unfailing Word of God. As Paul writes,

> Now may the God of hope [i.e., the God from Whom hope comes] fill you with every sort of joy and peace in

believing, so that you may have an abundance of hope by the power of the Holy Spirit (Rom. 15:13).

But how does the Holy Spirit generate this hope in the hearts of those who believe? Not in some mystical way, you can be sure. Paul had earlier addressed the matter:

Whatever was written before was written for our instruction that by the endurance and the encouragement that the Scriptures give us we may have hope (15:4).

Once again, we see that what in one place is attributed to the Holy Spirit in another is attributed to the Bible: hope comes from the Scriptures. The Holy Spirit, I remind you, works through the Bible, His own peculiar production. Because the Christian counselor has the Bible from which to counsel, he may give hope. Hope comes as the Holy Spirit enlightens believers to understand and trust the promises of God in Scripture.

An Important Warning

According to that modern Stoic Albert Ellis, if a person's thinking is right, his actions also will be right; so all we must do is straighten out the counselee's thinking. This idealistic viewpoint must be scrubbed at the beginning. There are many Christians who know perfectly well what they ought to do and how to do it but who disobey God anyway. They are led astray not by poor thinking, but by sinful desires (cf. James 1:14). In the return to rationalistic thought that I expect will soon overtake us, there will also be a return of the notion that education can answer all our problems. While biblical education is essential, there is of course more. A counselee must be willing to confess his sin, resist evil desires, and obey even when he does not feel like it. Willingness to do this depends on his willingness to ask the Spirit for help. Both Spirit-enlightened education and Spirit-motivated action are needed.

All the data in the world, correctly collated and categorized, are not enough. Counselees will say, "I know that," when you instruct them in God's will, but they do not obey. A person must be willing to submit to God and the Spirit's work, in spite of conflicting aspirations, ambitions, or desires.

The Spirit Who enlightens[3] is the same Spirit Who also "is producing in you both the willingness and the ability to do the things that please Him" (Phil. 2:13). The wisdom and the understanding, as critical as they are, do not accomplish God's will. Both the counselor and the counselee must ask God for the willingness and the ability to accomplish what they know He requires.[4] Teaching is but *one* of the four steps to change.

Since counseling is a matter of helping sinners from the inside out (see Matt. 15), it is a battle with obnoxious habits and ways of life that must be put off. This battle is waged not by education alone, but also by prayer, reproof, encouragement. We shall talk much more about that later when we discuss the other three steps of change and note how Romans 6–8 and Galatians 5 relate to spiritual warfare in counseling.

3. ". . . we haven't stopped praying for you and asking that you may be filled with the full knowledge of His will in all spiritual wisdom [i.e., wisdom which comes from the Spirit—through the Word of God, of course] and understanding" (Col. 1:9b).

4. Paul not only speaks of *knowing* God's will, thus setting our thinking straight (Phil. 3:15), but goes on to say, ". . . let us walk [live daily and habitually] according to the same level that we have attained" (3:16). Our intellectual attainments of the knowledge of God's will usually run ahead (often far ahead) of our actual daily walk. Paul says in effect, "Bring the two into conformity."

Ways to Emphasize God's Standards

Since those whom you counsel profess faith in Christ, they should have some acquaintance with and allegiance to the Scriptures as the standard for faith and practice.[5] A genuine commitment to Christ and His Word makes all the difference. You and your counselee start out with much in common, and you can be assured of the power and presence of the Holy Spirit to help you in all you do.

Early in counseling it is often wise to stress the Bible as the standard and the Holy Spirit as the power for change. That will give rise to a variety of responses, offering early clues as to the counselee's perspective and how to approach his case. While some counselees, perhaps many, will be encouraged by your reminder, others will object: "Yes, I thought that God was with me, but look at what happened." Still others, whose profession may be ingenuine, will voice confusion: "What do you mean? What are you talking about?" Given such responses, you know from the start whether you must explain your premise more fully and investigate more thoroughly your counselee's understanding and commitment. Counseling can proceed only inasmuch as both counselor and counselee acknowledge the Bible as the standard and the Holy Spirit as the Power behind all that goes on in counseling. So that is a good place to begin.

Sometimes counselees have their priorities scrambled. For instance, Tom says, "Pastor, I'll do anything to get my wife back!" Recognizing that he needs to be confronted

5. Remember, you should never counsel unbelievers. What they need is precounseling, or evangelism. On the other hand, if a counselee's profession of faith is false, proper counseling—insisting on doing God's will, even under threat of church discipline—ultimately will reveal the falsehood and will lead to repentance and faith or excommunication.

with a set of more biblical priorities, you respond,

"Anything?"

"Yes, that's what I said. I'll do anything to get her back."

"Would you lie, steal, commit murder?"

"Well, you know what I mean. . . ."

"No, I don't. But I'm trying to find out. Tell me, Tom, would you do what the Bible tells you to do *as a gimmick to get Flo back?*"

You see, many counselors would accept, even applaud, Tom's initial statement as evidence of great motivation. But though it is right for him to want Flo back, even a good priority can become a bad one when it is made the highest one. Tom's statement is out of line with biblical standards that forbid idolatry. His stated willingness to do "anything" to get his wife back indicates that he has put Flo before God and His standards, thus making her an idol. That misplaced priority must be corrected or all else will go wrong. If, for instance, Flo later returns, Tom might discontinue his changes because they are merely outward measures calculated *to get Flo back, not to please God.* Such retrogression is almost certain if his seeming advances are a gimmick to get what he wants rather than genuine conformity to God's will. And if she does not come back, you'd probably hear him say, "What's the use of continuing to do all of these things? It's not doing any good anyway; Flo has refused to return."

Tom needs to adopt pleasing God as his highest priority, *whether Flo returns or not.*[6] Only then will the changes he makes have value before God, remain in effect, and prepare him to face either contingency.

6. Counselors should be familiar with what the following verses say about pleasing God: John 8:29; Eph. 5:10; Col. 1:10; Heb. 11:6; 12:28; 13:16.

When God's standards are emphasized from the outset of counseling, particularly the first session, counseling gets off to a proper start. So look for an opportunity to emphasize that God's Word will be the standard for all that is done. You won't have to manufacture problems to find an opening. Enough issues will arise on their own for you to make the necessary point. Simply be aware of the need and seize the opportunity when it arises.

Let's talk about another example: Sam and Sally have marital problems. Apart from their attitudes, which you must deal with at the outset, you become aware of an issue that is a source of great controversy between them. Let us say, he wants to buy a sports car and she disapproves. How do they reach a solution? The counselor will tell them: "Sally, Sam, it doesn't matter what either one of you wants—it is what God wants that counts. Let's turn to His Word to discover the principles that apply to your problem."

One of the objections a non-Christian counselor constantly hears from one or another counselee is, "Well, you're just siding with him/her." If a counselee persists in that stance, the nonbelieving counselor, having no higher authority than himself to appeal to, cannot escape the charge. But the Christian counselor can say, "I don't intend to side with either of you; I intend to side with God. In the end, I think you will agree that means I am siding with both of you." The counselor can thereby teach both parties that whenever they reach an impasse because of conflicting wants, they should stop and ask, "But what does *God* want?"

Notice that the Christian counselor not only points to the standard, but also *makes a point of doing so*. In the long run, it is even more important for the counselee to grasp that

God's Word is the standard for life and for change than it is for him to be given a few isolated biblical principles for particular problems. Frequently counselors fail right here: they are too ready to solve a problem and move on. A few extra moments taken to emphasize that the Scriptures are practical, have answers, and ought to be used to solve problems in everyday affairs can pay dividends well worth the time and energy. Because few Christians use the Scriptures in daily matters nearly as much as they should, it is necessary to go the extra mile and *teach* them to do so. Good counselors never miss opportunities to teach such basic principles; that, along with explaining *how* the Bible is used to help, is one of the things that separate them from mediocre counselors.

Consider still another circumstance. Margie has sinned; she has lied to a friend about a boy they both like, in an effort to undermine her friend's interest in him. Not an uncommon situation. Margie is a Christian; her friend is not. Apart from other considerations (Is the boy a Christian?, etc., which we will eliminate to simplify the case), we can see once again how stressing the biblical standard can even help Margie to evangelize her friend. After careful instruction by the counselor, in which he may even act out an imaginary dialog with Margie's friend, this is how Margie's confession to Susan goes:

"I have something important to tell you, Susan."

"What's that?"

"I lied to you about Bob; he didn't really say what I told you he said. I was jealous of your interest in him and I tried to cut you out. It was wrong, and . . ."

"Why you twerp, how could . . ."

"Wait a minute, Susan, let me finish, please?"

"What you've got to say had better be good or *we'll* be 'finished' all right!"

"Susan, you know that I am a Christian, and . . ."

"There wasn't anything Christian about what you did . . ."

"I know it Susan; that's just the point. In the Bible God has forbidden me to lie and covet. I sinned. So, as the Bible teaches, I asked God's forgiveness . . ."

"What about mine? I . . ."

"I'm coming to that. In fact, that's exactly why I am here. But, first, let me tell you that even though it was probably the most embarrassing thing I have ever had to do, I went to Bob and explained that the reason you were giving him the cold shoulder is because of my lie. I asked his forgiveness too— just as I am asking yours right now. But I also want you to know that there is no way I could have told you or Bob had God not used the Bible to get under my skin and compel me to do it. Will you forgive me?"

The case speaks for itself. Margie's allegiance to a standard by which Christians live, God's standard, the Bible, has not only brought her to repentance and confession, and to seek forgiveness, but also shown Susan how a Christian handles sin. The next time Margie has an opportunity to witness to her, Susan may listen carefully to what the Bible says about Christ.

Again, the counselor has helped Margie do more than solve an isolated problem. He has so emphasized the practical use of God's standard that he has shown her how it may help her witness to her unsaved friend. Good counselors think of such things in counseling.

The Bible must not only be used up front in counseling; it must be *kept* before the counselee at all times as the basis for everything that is done. In no other way can the authority of

God and the help of the Holy Spirit in counseling be solidly established.

Assignment

Think of at least three other ways a counselor could stress to his counselees that the Bible is the standard. Write these out in brief vignettes similar to the episode involving Margie and Susan.

8

Teaching Biblical Principles

We come now to what may be the most interesting facet of teaching in counseling: teaching the principles that are critical to both immediate and lasting change. I stress that principles are essential to teaching lasting change, because many counselors focus only on immediate behavioral change, to the detriment of their counselees. Unless the counselee is taught not only how to get out of trouble, but also how to stay out of such trouble in the future, he (1) will be ripe for future failure, and (2) will develop a tendency to depend upon the counselor rather than upon God's truth and the Holy Spirit. Until the counselee himself knows in biblical terms the exact nature of his problem, how it developed, what God requires to solve it, how to avoid it in the future, and what to do if he should succumb to it again, he will forever be dependent upon someone else. Good, biblical counseling will not allow that to happen.

Teaching for the Long Haul

How do you help a counselee become dependent on God

and His Word, rather than on human counselors? How do you prepare someone for the long haul?

The counselor must make a conscious effort to do so. If he is unaware or unconvinced of the importance of teaching for the long haul, he will not foster dependence on God and His Word (and notice, I didn't say "independence" or Rogerian "autonomy"[1]). Counseling for the long haul is critical to all effective counseling (cf. I Pet. 4:1, 2).

That is why, for instance, Jesus taught frequently the doctrine of radical amputation (as I have called it—see *More Than Redemption* for details). Cutting off a right hand or foot or gouging out a right eye is a preventive measure, designed to deter repetition of a sin. It is a way of (1) preventing unconscious, automatic, habitual sin and (2) making it difficult to sin again in the same manner. As often as Jesus used the figure of radical amputation, it seems evident that He wished to impress upon us the urgency of taking radical measures to safeguard against sin. His mention of the possible necessity of losing the *right* (most valuable) eye, foot, or hand indicates the utter importance of avoiding sin. Indeed, Jesus treated the disregard for such precautions against future sin as indicative of an unrepentant and unsaved condition (note His strong words about being thrown into Gehenna: Matt 5:30b).

Some counselors have not thought through the importance of teaching for the long haul. Others, wishing to save

---

1. The goal of Rogerian counseling is "autonomy." From the garden of Eden, man was created a dependent creature. He was not given independence from God; indeed, it was his desire for independence that led him, and with him the entire human race, into sin. God created man with a need to depend on another (Himself). If he does not depend on God, therefore, man is sure to depend on someone else. That is why a proper dependence (not independence) *must be taught*. The goal of Rogerianism can never be achieved.

time, neglect such teaching and hope that the counselee's problem won't recur. The temptation is great for busy pastors to skimp by, doing as little as possible. Jesus' strong words should convince any conscientious counselor that teaching for the long haul is *necessary*. A small increase in time invested here will save him hours later, not to speak of averting untold suffering on the part of the counselee and those around him. Most important of all, it will guard against bringing dishonor upon God's Name from repeated sinful failure.

Another reason for failure to work for the long haul is that a counselee may be eager to end counseling at the first sign of relief. It is a natural reaction. When he goes to the dentist and finds relief from pain, he sees no reason to prolong an unpleasant experience. In some ways counseling is not unlike a series of visits to the dentist. Sin brings pain and suffering; that is its nature. And often relief comes only after a time of misery for the counselee. But when it is likely that a particular sin will recur and thereby reproduce the problem being dealt with, *the counseling must not stop at the arrival of relief*.

That fact must be deeply impressed upon the counselee. Otherwise he might simply not show up or might make excuses for not being able to come, in an attempt to cut off counseling. The best way I know to make the point is to read, explain, and apply (i.e., *teach*) the words of Jesus about radical amputation and the great need to take preventive measures against future sin. Ordinarily that will do the trick. Most counselees simply must be taught the reason for continuing and the benefits that continuation will bring. The fact to stress is that it is one thing to deal with the most recent occurrence of the sinful behavior, but still another to deal with the underlying pattern of which that behavior was but the most recent example. The basic pattern itself must be rooted out. Moreover, the counselee must understand that the counselor wants to help him become dependent on the Scriptures and the Holy Spirit rather than upon some expert. Learning to depend on God is a critical matter of growth, as well as a way of turning liabilities into assets.

With stubborn counselees who resist continuation, you may have to put the matter more strongly:

> John, I am not merely trying to prolong counseling. I don't want to do that any more than you do; my time is valuable too. But there is good reason for continuing a bit longer. Listen to what Jesus says about radical amputation. . . . Surely your insistence on ending counseling isn't indicative of your not caring whether you sin in the future; that would be evidence of an unregenerate condition. Unbelievers care only about getting relief from misery; genuine Christians care about glorifying their Father's Name.

Notice the counselor appeals not to his own authority or to what would please him. That must never happen. The appeal is to the authority of Christ. Since Christ said that avoiding recurrent sin calls for radical measures, the counseling must continue until the appropriate biblical principles and measures are understood. In order to accomplish all that the Bible requires of you as a counselor, you must persist in teaching its requirements to counselees.

The counselor holds no high and mighty stance as "The Expert." Rather, his appeal to the Scriptures and his eagerness to teach what the Scriptures say demonstrate that he also is under God's authority. He is to be heard not because he is the expert, but because he is a "man from God" with God's message in his mouth. Only the Christian counselor bears such an authority.

"The Expert" jealously guards his knowledge with a gnostic-like grasp, concealing it from the average man. Refusing to teach others, he would rather not divulge his secret to success. His esoteric and coded language and rituals (typical of physicians and psychotherapists) are calculated to enhance his authority and keep the rest of us peons in the dark. He is the opposite of what God's servant is to be. The work of the Christian counselor, like that of his Lord, is "not done in a corner." Far from minding that the counselee might understand the biblical dynamics involved in solving his problems, the godly counselor intently teaches him all about them. His concern is to make the counselee dependent not on him, but on God. He wants the counselee to act not on man's authority, but on the Lord's. In that way he differs radically from "The Expert."

The Christian counselor is to be an expert in one thing only: *in teaching counselees how to become more and more dependent on God and less and less dependent on anyone else. Like John the Baptist, he must become an expert in pointing counselees away from himself and to Christ. His is fundamentally a ministry of the Word.*[2]

---

2. The words *diakonia tou logou*, "the *ministry* of the Word," remind one of the duties of a domestic who goes about carrying out his or her chores. "Ministry" is a word not adequately understood. A *diakonos* was "one who waits on a table." It is possible that the word's etymology refers to "one who has come through the dust." In that sense, it is not far from our expression "one who does the dirty work." The notions of menial work are not altogether absent from it, but because of the dignity of the Word that is "served" in Christian counseling and preaching, the meaning of the term is modified and heightened, though never to the point of making the minister "the expert" or, as he is called in some traditions, the "Dominie" ("Lord"). Humility and willingness to give of oneself combined with expertise in teaching the Scriptures in a practical and authoritative manner (the authority always evidently God's) characterize the nice blend that inheres in the term as it is used by the New Testament writers.

That is why he must become an expert in Bible knowledge, interpretation, and exposition; and that is how he prepares to teach for the long haul. His goal is to help the counselee develop expertise in avoiding and handling future problems God's way.

Teaching Principles in Sessions for Immediate Results

It is time to put to rest the tawdry caricature of the nouthetic counselor[3] as someone who tears out passages of Scripture and hands them to counselees accompanied by the simplistic directions, "Take these three times a day with prayer." That is a cheap shot, and those who take the time to investigate the facts for themselves recognize it as both false and libelous, typical of the gossip against any progressive movement that violates the entrenched viewpoints of those with vested interests.

Over the years the leaders of nouthetic, or biblical, counseling have expended much effort to teach counselors how to use the Scriptures, emphasizing that inaccurate, unexplained, superficial, or unimplemented uses of the Scriptures demean God's Word and harm counselees. It is time to stress that again. Only here, let us do so more systematically, making clear how important such teaching is to productive, faithful, everyday counseling.

3. The word *nouthetic* comes from a Greek term *nouthesia*, used widely throughout the New Testament. The term is translated "counseling" in *The Christian Counselor's New Testament*, from which all New Testament quotations in this book are taken. It carries the meaning of change, out of concern, through confrontation. More about the word and its biblical usage may be found in *Competent to Counsel*. An organization bearing the name The National Association of Nouthetic Counselors certifies biblical counselors, counseling centers, and training centers. It may be contacted through the Christian Counseling and Education Foundation, 1790 E. Willow Grove Ave., Laverock, Pa. 19118.

Every counselee is entitled to an exposition of any passage to which his counselor refers. The exposition should be thorough enough for the counselee to see plainly that the command, promise, exhortation, encouragement, or whatever, is *from God* and not the invention of the counselor or anyone else. Nouthetic counselors often volunteer detailed explanation of a passage, or encourage counselees to ask for such exposition if there is the slightest doubt about the authority behind what a counselor has said. Such counselors want to emphasize that what matters is what God has said relevant to the case. No counselee is obliged to believe or do anything that cannot be supported biblically.

While such exposition must be thorough, it should not be bogged down with unessential details or sidelights having little to do with the counselee's problem. There is need for incisive yet concise exposition that demonstrates that the authority of the assertion is from God. That is the goal.

Let's consider an example. Suppose a counselee has questioned the assertion that his case, though serious, is by no means "hopeless." In response, the counselor may turn to I Corinthians 10:13 and explain how the promises of that verse apply to the counselee as a Christian. For instance, God has promised that no unique trial[4] has overtaken him. Indeed, the counselor will make the point that others have gone through similar trials successfully by God's help, contrary to the complaint of the counselee that his case is unique.

If necessary, the counselor will follow that explanation with the second assurance of the verse: that God vows, on the basis of His own "faithfulness," that the counselee will be subjected to no trial greater than his ability to withstand. A discussion may then ensue in which the counselor may

4. The counselor will make it clear that the word translated "temptation" in the King James Version means "trial" or "test" in this context.

need to drive home that the counselee is failing to endure his trial not because it is beyond his ability in Christ, but because he has not availed himself of Christ's strength for dealing with difficulty.

Further discussion may center on the third promise in the passage: that God in His time will remove him from the trial. This promise, God says, is made in order to generate hope, thereby enabling him to bear up under the trial while it lasts. The counselor, again, may have to point out that the counselee's attitude of hopelessness is a direct denial of the Word of God, is bound to fail, and must be changed.

The Christian counselor works carefully through the verse, comparing and contrasting the attitudes and behavior of the counselee with the truth in the verse, thus encouraging him with biblical hope. He knows that there is no hope in empathetic agreement, but only in empathetic disagreement in which he looks more deeply into the counselee's problem than does the counselee himself—deeply enough to see God's viewpoint on the matter. Because hope comes from doing what the Bible requires, the counselor will never allow the counselee to shirk his responsibilities, no matter how difficult, but will insist that the promises of God leave him neither hopeless nor helpless if he obeys God. To remind the counselee of what he has been told, the counselor may want to give him a copy of the booklet *Christ and Your Problems*, which is a pointed exposition of the same verse.

Space is limited here, but in actual counseling the specific implications of the principles of I Corinthians 10:13 and other verses would be worked out. The counselee would be shown exactly how God applies the truth of the passage to his situation, even to the point of specific implementation.

As you can see, that is not handing out verses like prescriptions. It is bringing the counselee to grips with the implications of the Bible for his situation.

Let's take another example, to show how the Bible is used to clarify the counselee's problem, in contrast to the confusing, hope-destroying constructs of psychotherapy. A counselee has presented his problem as a lack of a good self-image. He claims that others, by demeaning him, have created in him a basic negative outlook that hampers him and prevents him from finding or holding a job.

How does a biblical counselor confront him with Scripture? His concern will be first of all to sweep aside the modern, erroneous, unbiblical views of self-worth and self-image that have become this counselee's excuse for failure. In order to do so, he might approach the counselee as follows:

"Frank, you tell me your problem is a basic lack of self-esteem?"

"Right, Pastor; that's what my psychotherapist, Dr. Abe M. Slow, says. I am suffering from low self-esteem because of the way others have put me down over the years. There was my mother. . . ."

"I see. Well, tell me, where in the Bible do you find anything about needing high self-esteem to obey God's commandment to work?"

"Well . . . I don't know; but that's what Dr. Slow told me."

"Let's forget about what Dr. Slow said for a while and look at what God says instead. After all, God, not Dr. Slow, is the One Who made you; He should know something about what makes you tick, don't you think?"

"Well . . . yeah, sure, but. . . ."

"In the Bible we are told a number of important things about the self. For instance, the Gospels assure us that unless we deny (literally 'say no to') self and crucify self (that is what taking up the cross daily means) and follow Christ, we cannot truly serve Him (Luke 9:23-27). Moreover, rather than pamper self, we are told that 'whoever wants to save his life will lose it, but whoever loses his life for My sake will find it' (Matt. 16:25). Surely there is something wrong with Dr. Slow's teaching! Nowhere in all of the Bible is there even the slightest hint that good self-esteem is necessary for obedience; everywhere, instead, God calls us sinners, enemies, etc. Do you think He would 'put us down' that way if lowering our self-esteem made us incapable of following His commands?"

"Well, it doesn't seem so. . . ."

"No, it doesn't. As a matter of fact, there is no way to serve Him faithfully until we recognize that, in ourselves, we are nothing more than rebellious sinners in His sight. Only when we are willing to admit (unlike the Pharisee and like the publican) that we are sinners who can ask for nothing but mercy, are we ready to serve Christ properly. Presumably Dr. Slow doesn't know these facts and is resting instead on the ideas of men."

"Well, I guess that's true, but how can God help me? What must I do?"

"You are a Christian. Now, confess your self-centeredness and your failure to obey God's commandment to labor six days a week, and then begin to search for a job. If you allow the negative comments of others to get you down, that is your fault. You are responsible to God, not to them. You may think that you don't have a job, but you do. God gave you one: to work six days. Spend five days, eight hours a day looking for a job, use the other day for work you must do around the house, and I can almost guarantee you that you will find a job in a couple of weeks. Now, let's talk about how one goes about applying for a job. . . ."

The exchange above is only a slimmed-down sample of what such counseling is like, focusing on the counselor's part to illustrate the teaching of biblical principles in counseling. Obviously, not every counselee will acquiesce so easily. Often the struggle will be longer and harder, requiring more Scripture and closer exegesis. And the counselee will have much more to say;[5] indeed, if he doesn't, the counselor will probe his thinking and attitudes. He will want to know whether the counselee really understands the problem scripturally, accepts the biblical solution to it, and is willing to follow it.

Since the counselor not only must use the Bible in counseling, but also must be able to teach it, he must know it, in one respect, better than the preacher. Unlike the man in the pulpit, who has had time to prepare what he will say, the counselor must handle whatever comes his way, never knowing beforehand where any given session may take him. His knowledge of the Bible must have both breadth and depth. In arguing from the Scriptures, as he must frequently do, he must have a grasp on the passage that will enable him to explain and apply it in detail when necessary. Can you see now why he must devote himself wholly to the study of the Word?

Assignment

Together with a couple of other students, choose and develop a case from *The Christian Counselor's Casebook* that demonstrates the need for both breadth and depth in the use of Scripture. The case will be role-played in class. Be ready to explain and defend what you have done.

5. The counselee will be encouraged to speak so that the counselor may gauge his acceptance and understanding of the Scriptures. But because the biblical counselor has God's truth to teach, he will at times command the floor.

9

Teaching in the Milieu

Teaching in Preaching and Counseling

As a teacher, the counselor has one great advantage over the preacher: the counselor teaches in the milieu. (In other ways preachers have the advantage, but that's not the point here.)

Just what do I mean by teaching "in the milieu"? Let me share an experience. Once, when I was in the pastorate, I preached from John 1:1. I happened to comment for five minutes or so on how the Jehovah's Witnesses misinterpret that verse and how we should respond to their misinterpretation. Monday morning I received an urgent telephone call from a member of the congregation.

"Pastor, can you tell me what to say to a Jehovah's Witness about John 1:1?"

"Brenda, you were in church yesterday when I spoke about that very problem."

"Oh I know, Pastor, but one came to the door this morning."

Teaching in the milieu, addressing the actual situations people are facing, makes a great difference. Sometimes a preacher may be able to capitalize on such a circumstance (e.g., a major news story that has stirred the congregation, such as an attempted assassination of the President), but usually he must labor to involve everyone. He must *create* a milieu for what he has to say. That is why it is gratifying to a pastor when members of the congregation say things like, "That sermon was for me; it really spoke to my situation." Yet, seldom does everyone in a congregation feel that way.

Because of the individualized nature of the counseling context, however, you are always getting down to concrete particulars of the counselee's present circumstance. In counseling, you teach in the milieu.

Two major benefits arise out of teaching in the milieu:

1. People learn better, faster, more eagerly.
2. People are able to put what they learn into practice immediately because they are learning for doing.[1]

The first benefit is self-evident. The incident related at the beginning of the chapter tells the whole story. It vividly points up the difference between Greek "academic" learning and biblical learning in the milieu. On Monday, the woman was eager to learn what to say to a Jehovah's Witness because she had one on the string—he was coming back in a couple hours, and she wanted to be ready for him. But the day before, in church, the idea of a Jehovah's Witness ever coming to her door seemed so remote that the explanation of John 1:1 didn't even phase her; it went in one ear and out the other. She wasn't interested. Incidentally, I learned something from that experience (out of that milieu):

1. I am not advocating learning *by* doing but learning *for* doing; that is, learning for use. John Dewey, who taught learning by doing, was wrong. His optimistic, humanistic theology, which was akin to that of Carl Rogers, considered man good and therefore capable of determining what is best for himself. Dewey did not believe in revelation or authoritative teaching. The biblical method, learning for doing, requires counselors and all Christian teachers to teach "to *observe*," that is, to "obey" God's holy Word.

my task is to *make* such information vital and relevant when preaching. (Now, if I suspect it is necessary, I often say something like this: "I'm about to tell you something that you may think is unimportant. But before you tune me out, let me tell you about a woman just like you. I was preaching on John 1:1. . . .) Moreover, I must create a mental milieu for the truth that I am about to teach. But that has to do with preaching.

The second great benefit is that a counselee can turn doctrine into life *as a part of the teaching process*. The goal of all teaching in the Scriptures, as we have seen, is to change people, to help Christians to move closer to God. So often that change does not take place because biblical doctrine is taught merely as a fact to be known and not as truth to be lived. Even when it is taught as fact that affects everyday living, if there is no opportunity to use the truth, the teaching will probably not be transferred from the mind to the hands, the feet, and the mouth. Again, an aside for the preacher: whenever possible, you should point out the danger of merely intellectualizing about the truth, and you should direct your congregation to areas in which they may immediately begin to transform a truth into life. In this regard, Colossians 1:9-10 is the preacher's byword. He teaches truth *in order* to change lives in ways that please God.

Assuming, for the moment, that the counselee wants to change, you must help him to take what he has been taught in the counseling session and use it during the following week at work, at his home—i.e., in the milieu. Then, when he returns for the next counseling session, he and you should discuss how well he did, correct any misconceptions that have surfaced, work on skills, and plan how to make the next week a success. Frequently the main causes of failure are not misconceptions, but sinful attitudes or poor skills in relating to others. Such problems emerge vividly in the milieu.

Skills, such as how to communicate with others and how to seek a job, and proper attitudes can be taught and formed for life only in the milieu.[2] But that will be discussed in detail later, under step four, "Disciplined Training in Righteousness."

Since counselees do not always recognize the importance of what you are teaching them, you must make plain its experiential importance. Otherwise they will learn no more quickly than the woman who failed to hear my words about John 1:1. Much like the preacher who must create a mental milieu, you will say such things as this: "I know that you don't see the immediate importance of learning how to control anger, but it is vital to your situation. Let's rehearse how you are going to face your boss and ask his forgiveness for your sin. I'll be the boss and respond to you as perhaps he would. Try to recognize how you would be tempted to lose your temper, and practice responding as a Christian should." In other words, you will tell the counselee that he is learning *for future doing*. There soon will be a milieu in which he may very well have to use the teaching and the skills you are now urging him to learn. Role playing in a makeshift milieu teaches him many of the dynamics that will arise in actual encounters with his boss.

---

2. Try to teach someone to swim, to play football, or to paint pictures from a book! Ordinarily, persons should be counseled only when living in their own milieu. To remove someone from his everyday life for the period of time during which he is being counseled is like draining the water from the pool.

Learning under Pressure

Counselees benefit from the pressure of learning in the milieu. But often there is no such pressure when someone is learning for the long haul, as important as that is. You may therefore have to *structure* experiences that create pressure to learn. Take the following counseling case for example:

"Well, John, you finally have got that debt paid off. That's just great! You have a lot to thank God for; His biblical stewardship principles were effective, weren't they?"

"They sure were, pastor. I feel so much better now I can hardly stand it! And it will be great to be able to end counseling too."

"Do you think you are ready?"

"Well, the debt is paid."

"Yes, but do you think that in the future, if things get tight again, you will be able to refrain from spending money you don't have?"

"Well, I don't know. Anyway, I don't have to think about that. Now that the debt is paid, I've got a good bit of discretionary money again."

"Yes, but that is the point; we don't know what you will do under pressure. You're thankful to God for getting you out of debt, aren't you?"

"I sure am."

"Well, I have a suggestion that will kill two birds with one stone. For the next two months, why don't you commit yourself to some Christian organization and promise to send all of your discretionary money—a definite sum— each week to them. Then you can see if you have really learned to live within your budget and not run up charges that you cannot pay without a mammoth effort like the one we have just made. You can express your thanks to God by giving, and you can begin to put into practice the preventive stewardship principles about which we have been speaking. In this way, those principles will become real to you, a part of your life. The organization will hold you to your commitment, so that you cannot fudge on it, and you will be able to practice living within your means during tight circumstances. Is there some group to which you have always wanted to contribute?"

Note that the counselor structures the milieu in such a way that the counselee need not wait for further pressures before he can begin to learn experientially how to face those pressures.

Milieu Teaching Is Not Optional

Teaching in the milieu is God's method of teaching. He Himself uses it, and He enjoins us to do so too. When He gave directions for teaching children in a way that would "deeply impress" His truth upon their hearts (Deut. 6:7), He commanded teaching in the milieu. That is clear from Deuteronomy 6:1-9,20-25 and 11:18-20 (study these verses in the Berkeley Version). There He says that teaching should be done when sitting at home, while walking on the road, when lying down, and when getting up. In other words, everywhere, day and night, in the actual milieu of daily living.[3]

Moreover, in those same passages, we see how God Himself structured a milieu that recalled and helped to recreate a previous one. God commanded "laws and

3. For more on this, see my book, Back to the Blackboard (Phillipsburg, N.J.: Presbyterian and Reformed, 1982).

ordinances" that raised questions in the minds of children subjected to them. When they asked what the laws and ordinances meant, their parents were required to teach them about the deliverance from Egypt. The laws and ordinances *created* a teaching milieu, as did the yearly passover feast.

Many Bible students seem perplexed that God did not give them a book in which all of His teachings are set forth in the academic manner, as in modern textbooks. It disturbs them that they must abstract truth from situations, that is, from the cultural milieu of the biblical record.[4] But God taught truth in the milieu because He did not want us to dichotomize truth and life. Truth is to be "observed"; it is for living, for pleasing God. We can learn much by simply observing how God teaches in His own Word. If we do not, we shall never learn to teach well ourselves.

Restructuring a Milieu

A person need not always be in a milieu himself to benefit from it. He can vicariously benefit from the experiences of others. That is what I Corinthians 10:13 is all about (reread that verse along with its immediate context). Preachers,

4. Some academes have called this teaching method "pretheoretical" and have dubbed God's biblical approach "naive." Saying that there is no theology in the Scriptures, they mistake the value and the place of both modern and biblical methods. Paul was surely a great theologian. The Bible is not pretheoretical at all; it is posttheoretical. In it, carefully conceived theology is artfully applied to life in language understandable to all (not merely to the scientific community). Though Paul's approach (and that of the other New Testament writers) is not essentially Greek, with the systematic analysis of the academy, one must *not* think it to be atheological. The practical, life-application and more holistic approach to theology found in the Scriptures is what many of our churches lack.

however, have been taught to preach by the lecture-rather-than-preaching method (for a full discussion of this see my book, *Preaching with Purpose*). Until they dump this unbiblical and counterproductive method of "preaching," their teaching will be academic and cut off from the benefits of the milieu, in-ministry method. They must learn, when preaching or counseling, to teach people the way they learn best (or perhaps exclusively)—in a milieu, whether real or vicarious. The preacher must learn to "preach up" a vicarious milieu for the truth, always suggesting to his listeners previously unrecognized ways of incorporating the truth into the milieu of each person's life at the moment.

Detecting Problems by Milieu Teaching

When a counselee fails between sessions to do all he was assigned by way of homework, problems that otherwise might have gone undetected virtually leap out of the milieu to throttle him. That is one reason why the counselor gives homework.[5] His first interest, of course, is to help the counselee solve problems through putting faith into practice. Secondly, he wants the counselee to learn through practice how to put off the old ways and put on new ones. But, thirdly, and of only slightly less importance, he wants to uncover any remaining difficulties. This he can do in no better way than by observing the results of the counselee's efforts in the milieu.[6]

5. Homework is vitally important. I have discussed it in detail in *The Christian Counselor's Manual* and see no value in repeating that material here. Homework is based on the idea that faith should lead to works, truth to life, and repentance to its appropriate fruit.

6. I have not mentioned data gathering. Because it is so important to fulfilling the requirements of Prov. 18:13, 15, 17, I have devoted several chapters to it in *The Christian Counselor's Manual*. I shall also consider data gathering and change in chapter 13, under step two, "Conviction."

Milieu Teaching Is Basic

Helen Keller is a dramatic example of learning from the milieu. Blinded and deafened by disease at the age of 19 months, she was for years cut off from the world around her. It seemed she was doomed to remain that way; how could anyone get through to her? Academes could not. But Annie Sullivan did. By running cold water over one of Helen's hands and spelling the word *water* in Helen's other hand, Sullivan finally broke through the barrier. Her method was absolutely basic and is a perfect demonstration of learning through the milieu.

How else could a counselor better become a more effective teacher than by following God's own method for teaching truth? How else can he be obedient if he does not? He must learn to teach in the milieu. But how will he learn? Obviously, there is but one way—the counselor too must learn in the milieu.

That means you should take the advice found in this chapter and apply it immediately to your present counseling cases. Ask yourself, "Am I teaching in the milieu? Could my counseling be more effective if I knew of ways to do so, or if I created a milieu for my counselees to test their progress and to practice God's new ways?" If, in answer to those questions, you discover that there is work to be done, you will be experiencing the pressure of the milieu, and you will doubtless learn how to do what we have been talking about much more effectively than if you keep on trying to learn about it in an "academic" manner. So, get with it!

Assignment

In a paper of no more than six pages, describe four counseling situations in which teaching in the milieu would be helpful. Write out the situations as short vignettes. Think of the pressure of the milieu as an incentive for learning.

10

How to Teach

In addition to teaching in the milieu, there are several other important keys to knowing how to communicate truth in the counseling context.

Personal Involvement

The counselor-as-teacher must become personally involved with counselees. Freud taught just the opposite, and since his time the medical model that has wrongly been associated with counseling has perpetuated his idea of disengagement. We know, however, that such disengagement is wrong when we read Paul's words in II Corinthians 11:23-29. After cataloging an amazing list of sufferings for Christ, Paul concludes by saying,

> And besides these outward trials, there is the daily burden of oversight that grows out of my concern for all of the churches. Who is weak, and I am not weak? Who stumbles, and I am not upset? (vv. 28, 29).

Those words describe a very involved man! Paul identified

himself so closely with particular members of congregations, that he felt their weaknesses and their hurts. He wept
with those who wept and rejoiced with those who rejoiced
(Rom. 12:15). In one place, he went so far as to say,

> I shall mourn over many of those who have sinned
> before and haven't repented of the uncleanness and
> sexual sin and sensualness that they have practiced
> (II Cor. 12:21b).

You have a choice in your counseling practice. You can
emulate the cold, white-coated "professional" counselor or
the warm, caring apostle who told us to follow his example
in ministry (I Cor. 11:1; Phil. 4:9). Will you pursue the
biblical approach or the modern substitute for it? If you
want to teach biblically, you must become involved.

"But my personality is different. I'm not the sort of person who gets very deeply involved with others," you object. That may be true, but your personality isn't set in
concrete; it can be changed. Look how Christ changed
Peter's personality. Yours can change too. Indeed, unless it
does, you will continue to be ineffective in the ministry,
especially in the ministry of counseling. You will have to
learn how to let your emotions go, and, probably through
earnest prayer for each counselee, how to carry others'
burdens the way Paul did.[1]

By carrying others' burdens (cf. Gal. 6:2: "Bear one an-

---

1. It is not a matter of "manufacturing" or affecting emotions. As in all
genuine ministry, the ministry of the Word in counseling must be from the
heart; it must be something *already felt within*. Content should determine
style, as in preaching. One's manner with a counselee must grow out of
the content of (1) the situation, (2) the information exchanged in discussion, and (3) what God says about both in His Word. And this manner
must be appropriate; appropriate emotion is neither contrived nor stifled.
Manner should always *serve* matter. But it must serve as a willing servant.
That is why involvement is so important in teaching.

other's burdens and so fulfill Christ's law") Paul meant having a concern for them that leads to sharing in their problems. Christ's "law," which is fulfilled by this burden bearing, is the command to love. Because this obligation is laid on every Christian in Galatians 6:2, a context that enjoins counseling on every Christian (about which see *Ready to Restore* [Phillipsburg, N.J.: Presbyterian and Reformed, 1981]), you are obligated to love your counselees by bearing their burdens. You too must carry the weight of their troubles. You cannot say that failure to do so is a matter of indifference, or one in which personality differences excuse you. If your personality is a drawback, then it must be changed.

If your personality conflicts with this biblical concern for others, you are probably too concerned about yourself. Such self-concern is sin. You will see a change in your personality when you begin thinking and praying more about your counselees. Do not set out to change your personality directly. That itself is a selfish pursuit. When you jettison your self-concern (whether in the form of fear of people or a self-centeredness in which you put your affairs first), your personality will change as a by-product. In Philippians 2:3, 4 Paul gives the basic directions you need to change as a person, the "put ons" by which you must actively work at putting others and their interests before your own. When you do this prayerfully and regularly, not only in counseling but also in every area of your daily life, you will discover that you have become a new person with, as a result, a new personality to boot.

Involvement is important in teaching because people are people, not things. The ordinary person doesn't get involved with chairs, walls, desks, etc. When someone does, we send him for counseling! We become involved with *persons*—God and our neighbors. And the involvement that the Bible requires is an involvement of love. All of the Bible can be summed up in this: it teaches us how to love God and our neighbor. That is what Jesus said. And love, as Paul tells us, requires you to carry the burdens of others in order to restore them.

You recognize that involvement is essential when you read James 1:7: "That person shouldn't suppose that he will receive anything from the Lord." About whom is he speaking? The double-minded man (cf. v. 8). The trouble with a double-minded doubter is that he does not become fully involved with God. He is like the man at the baseball game who rooted for both teams with equal enthusiasm. At the seventh-inning stretch someone behind him asked, "How is it that you root so vigorously for both teams?" The man replied, "I'm a farmer. I live way out in the country and get to a ball game only once a year. When I do, I'm going to be sure that I'm on the winning side." You can't take that attitude toward God; you must be whole-hearted in your relationship with Him. God will not have you share your concern for Him with a concern for someone or something else (cf.I Kings 18:21). He will not allow you to hedge your bets. He demands complete involvement. That is the way of love. And that is how you must become involved with your counselee.

A counselee knows when his counselor cares enough to be involved. When the counselor sweats over problems with his counselees, he knows that he is involved enough to give not only his wisdom, but something of himself. That was the way Paul and his companions ministered:

> You know that like a father dealing with his children, we urged and encouraged and charged each one of you to walk in a manner that is worthy of God (I Thess. 2:11, 12).

What did a fatherly ministry require? We discover the answer in verse 8:

> We were so concerned for you that we were glad to give you, not only God's good news, but also a part of our very souls—because you became so dear to us.

There is no way you can escape the force of such statements. Paul gave of himself in a personal counseling ministry (to "each one"). Much counseling done today—even by those whose basic biblical orientation is correct—shows little "concern" or "burden." There is no "weeping" and seldom any "rejoicing." The teaching is purely academic, producing a response equally academic!

When people know you love them and care enough to give yourself to them, they listen to what you have to say, and that has an effect on both their living and thinking. So, the first element in proper teaching is to truly have the welfare of the counselee in mind.

Enthusiasm

Christ told the church at Laodicea, "You are neither cold nor hot (I wish you were cold or hot). . . . because you are lukewarm, and neither cold nor hot, I am going to vomit you out of my mouth" (Rev. 3:15, 16). In those words He expressed a very important principle: lack of enthusiasm is sickening. It is revolting and disgusting. If you want to turn off your counselee, then teach him blandly. Be lukewarm about what you have to say, be "clinical" and "professional," and you will fail to teach. What people respond to is teachers who teach with enough conviction to get their listeners stirred up about what they have to say.

Sometimes a counselor's genuine enthusiasm for a biblical truth is bottled up behind a rigid, formal personality.

Once again, if your personality is in the way, then it must be changed! You must work at letting your emotions show and expressing your feelings openly, both in good preaching and in good counseling.

But often the problem is that God's truth does not grip the counselor. That too is a spiritual problem and must be dealt with in terms of repentance and change. You must discover exactly why the truth does not move you. Have you become so familiar with it that you have allowed familiarity to breed contempt? Have you become "professionalistic" so that you treat God's Word as but an instrument in your hands? What is the source of the lukewarmness? No mere technique will solve a spiritual problem between you and God. You must discover what is wrong, repent, and correct your ways. In other words, the process of changing others often demands, first of all, changes in the counselor.

Enthusiasm can make a great difference in a counseling session. Often a counselee's hope depends upon the counselor's expressed attitude. Take the following dialog as an example in which the counselor turns despair into hope by enthusiasm:

"Well, I blew it this week, Pastor. I simply couldn't follow the assignment you gave me."

"Great!"

"Great? What do you mean 'great'? I thought you'd be all over me for failing."

"Well, I don't mean that failure is great in and of itself, of course; what I have in mind is that this specific failure provides us with a recent case in which we can closely explore and understand the reason for your general failure. This is what I have been waiting for! I wouldn't be a bit surprised if we find, embedded in this current failure, the very data for which we have been searching for two weeks."

Enthusiasm for God's truth, of course, may not all be upbeat. If a counselee refuses to repent of a sin, the counselor may well have to wax warm about the virtues and the effectiveness of church discipline! Not that he talks about it with a fiendish glee; what I mean is that he *conveys conviction* that church discipline works, and that he will apply it to the full because Christ has ordered him to do so. Inasmuch as Christ initiated discipline to change people, the counselor does not hesitate to use it. He disciplines enthusiastically, in hope, because he expects things to happen through church discipline, and everything in his words, demeanor, and voice indicates that fact. In other words, what I have called "enthusiasm" includes a transparency on the counselor's part, in which he communicates exactly what he thinks and believes—with conviction. To use the Lord's figure of speech, he is "hot" about what he has to say.

Color and Vividness

The use of examples, colorful vocabulary, and illustrations is just as vital in counseling as it is in preaching. Because so much has been said about this in the preaching manuals, I shall not discuss it here in any depth.[2] I do want to note, however, the importance and use of illustrations, color, and vividness in counseling.

Fundamentally, there are four uses of examples or incidents or illustrations in counseling:

1. To clarify
2. To make memorable
3. To demonstrate how something may be done.
4. To encourage

2. If you are interested in what I have to say on the subject, see my books on preaching.

Illustrations clarify ideas. If a counselee doesn't understand what you are saying (you would be wise to anticipate this), you will need to *illustrate* or, as that word means, *throw light on* the point you wish to make.

Let me illustrate: Suppose a counselor has been trying to teach his counselee the impossibility of proceeding further with counseling unless some complicating problems are settled. The counselee doesn't understand. The counselor may then say,

> Well, it's something like this: If I got a tangle in my fishing line and, in trying to untangle it, put three new knots in the line, I'd have to untie those three knots first before I could get back to the original one. That is what has happened in your case. In attempting to untangle the original problem, you have put three new knots in your line.

Many people who come for counseling don't easily grasp what the counselor is saying. If they are jaded by their problems and do not think as swiftly in counseling sessions as they otherwise might, they need vivid illustrations to help them see clearly the point the counselor is making.

Illustrations, examples, and vivid language also make points memorable. The counselor will find himself telling a counselee from time to time, "Whenever you are tempted to do that again, think of the garbage can." Having given an illustration about a garbage can in a way that struck the counselee with force, the counselor ties that illustration in with an assignment for the future. Just the mention of a garbage can brings back the point of the illustration with much the same impact it initially had on him.

One of the reasons Jesus' teaching sticks in our minds is that He regularly illustrated truth and used graphic language. Even small phrases like "the bread of life," "the door," and the other "I am" statements demonstrate this fact. Notice too, how Jesus used these materials not only in preaching to the crowds but also in speaking to individuals (e.g., Nicodemus: "born again," "the wind blows where it wants to . . ."; the woman at the well: "the water of life," etc.).

A third use of illustrative material is to show concretely how something must be done. Here case studies may be useful. Of course all of the rules for flattening out case studies, so that the persons about whom you are speaking are utterly unidentifiable, must be observed.[3] The counselor may find himself frequently saying things like this:

> In a situation not unlike yours, this is what I told another counselee to do. [He then describes the interview.] The man went and did [so-and-so], and here is what happened. [He describes the results.] In your case it would work much the same way, the only differences being. . . .

Then, too, illustrative material can be used effectively to encourage and motivate. In accordance with I Corinthians 10:13, examples of others whom Christ has brought through similar situations can be of enormous help and encouragement. Again, the rules for flattening out case histories should be observed rigidly. On the other hand, instances describing the consequences of disobeying biblical directives also help to motivate as they did in the books of Jude and II Peter.

Like your Lord, you must learn to use illustrations, examples, and vivid language effectively; perhaps no other technique for teaching is of greater importance.

---

3. To "flatten out" a case, eliminate times, places, names, and unique events or facts that would identify those involved. Changes not affecting the point may be made to further mask the real person.

Printed and Other Aids

Counselors of the Rogerian and Freudian schools have not thought much about teaching methods, simply because they do not teach. As a result, many counselors who have been trained in those schools of thought know little about teaching aids. Let me, therefore, mention some of the aids that have been used successfully for teaching purposes in counseling.

Pamphlets, booklets, books, and other written materials may of course be useful as handouts to accompany counseling. The pamphlet series that I had published and the small books *Four Weeks with God and Your Neighbor*, *How to Handle Trouble*, and *How to Overcome Evil* were all designed for such a purpose.[4] Many other giveaways have been found helpful. Every pastor should ask his church to provide a fund for purchasing supplies of handout materials.

In addition to these materials, desk-top turnover charts and chalkboards (or white boards on which you write with felt-tip pens) are very useful for in-session instruction. Prepared materials on turnover charts indicate that the dynamics appropriate to one's case are common enough to be put into permanent form. This tends to give hope in line with the encouraging promise of I Corinthians 10:13a. Rub off "transfer" letters may be used to make charts that look professional.

Other useful aids include overhead projectors, audio tape recordings, video tape recordings, homework sheets, instruction sheets, and the like. Sometimes visual and audible aids provide a way of calling in a second witness to reinforce points made by the counselor. Just hearing a biblical truth

4. Available from Presbyterian and Reformed Publishing Co., Phillipsburg, N.J.

in a different form or from another person can make a difference.

Obviously, this brief survey of the methods of teaching in counseling is merely suggestive. Its purpose is to stimulate your thinking and call you to innovate. Are you using any of these teaching methods in your counseling? Perhaps you are using others that have not been mentioned. But perhaps you could improve your teaching along these lines. Why not give it some thought?

Without love for the counselee, any method or technique will fail. But with love, you can succeed even without aids. Love that leads to involvement and enthusiasm for what God can do, bolstered by faithful prayer for counselees, is what makes vivid language, illustrations, techniques, and aids truly useful. Without such love, they are but a clanging gong!

Assignment

1. In the space below, develop a list of other teaching aids that have not been mentioned in this chapter.

_____

_____

_____

_____

_____

_____

_____

_____

_____

_____

_____

2. Write up an imaginary dialog in which you show how enthusiasm, involvement, or illustrative material could aid the counseling-teaching process.

PART III

STEP TWO,
CONVICTION

11

The Role of Conviction in Counseling

It isn't easy to find a chapter on conviction in a counseling textbook. That may be one reason why the counseling in so many textbooks proves to be inadequate. According to God's program of *nouthetic*, or admonitory, counseling, conviction is an essential step. That is because men are born in sin, which thoroughly affects their lives. The step in the ministry of the Word that Paul calls "conviction," therefore, presupposes the need for bringing counselees to an acknowledgment of their failure to meet the standards (teachings) of God's Word.

Conviction is the second step in the process of change because conviction follows an awareness of God's requirements. The logic of that priority is apparent; in actual practice, however, there are times when conviction and teaching go hand in hand. So we must not think of them as mutually exclusive. In order to produce conviction, one may have to teach new material or reteach in new ways what the counselee has heard but has not yet converted from theory to practice. The counselor may need to further clarify biblical truth and how it applies to the particulars of his counselee's situation. The Bible requires the counselor to learn skills in using the Word of God in order to bring about conviction.

I can almost hear some of you saying, "Come on, Adams, you know that conviction is the work of the Holy Spirit. What are you talking about? I just minister the Word and let the Holy Spirit do the convicting." Well of course the Holy Spirit convicts; about that there can be no doubt or compromise. Nonetheless, in II Timothy 3 and elsewhere (e.g., James 2:9) we are told also that the *Scriptures* convict men of sin. And in II Timothy 4:2b, which closely follows the four-step passage, II Timothy 3:16, Paul commands the *minister of the Word* to "convict, reprove and urge. . . ." Here, as you can see, it is not enough to say, "I just minister the Word and let the Holy Spirit do the convicting." The minister of the Word himself is required to "convict." And there are other passages to the same effect.[1] That means *bringing conviction to counselees itself is a part of the ministry of the Word*. The matter is not quite so simple as at first it might seem. It is important to bear in mind always the relationship of the human and the divine in the ministry of the Word.

Putting all three elements together, we see that the *Word* is *ministered* properly only when it is ministered in the power of the *Holy Spirit* with a view to bringing conviction. We neglect any of the three elements only at the peril of the counselee.

So I shall discuss all three aspects of the ministry of

1. See also I Tim. 5:20; Titus 1:9. Opposite views are popularly entertained. In a recent book by Bea Fosmire, entitled *Growing Pains* (Grand Rapids: Zondervan, 1983), for.instance, human agency is denied. Attempting to convict another is denounced as helping the Holy Spirit along (p. 67), and we are told that this work "belongs to God alone" (p. 68).

conviction, but with emphasis on the use of the Word by the human minister, since the Spirit's ministry is according to His sovereign will and cannot be manipulated by men. The counselor is neither to attempt what the Spirit alone can do, nor even to attempt his own rightful ministry without the Spirit's approval and blessing. Suffice it to say here that the minister convicts others effectively only by the Spirit's power. He is thereby the Spirit's minister.[2]

Before proceeding further, it may be worthwhile to note that some counseling does not require conviction. At times a counselee may merely need information or help in decision making. Such data and direction will help him grow and avoid potential problems. Paul calls this simply "teaching." The bulk of the ordinary counseling you do, however, is occasioned by sinful practices, attitudes, and decisions. The same was true in Paul's day. In all such counseling, conviction is a critical factor in bringing about change.

But why is conviction so important? Because it pertains to the counselee's relationship to God. Much change that is offered today in counseling—even in the Name of Christ—is sub-Christian. Aimed at little more than making counselees happier, it neglects the basic reason why a believer must change: to please God. As if God's glory were of secondary importance, His Name's sake is omitted from the picture, out of deference to better health or a more smoothly running marriage. Such considerations, not wrong in themselves, are quite wrong when they are not subordinated to the greater purpose of pleasing and honoring God.

In convicting us of sin, God is calling on us to recognize that the change we must make is not simply good advice; it

2. In discussing the convicting work of the Spirit, we should note that He not only calls men to this ministry by His Word but sets them apart to it, gifts them for it, directs them in it, and blesses their work. In every sense of the term they are *His* ministers.

is an imperative. He is telling us that what we have done is not merely inconvenient, counterproductive, or undesirable; it is flat wrong and *must* be changed. Conviction, therefore, brings a dimension to change that is otherwise lost.

Moreover, by requiring conviction, God is saying that He cares about us. Unlike the father who lets his child's disobedience slip by unmentioned, God shows concern enough to convict, to go to the trouble of arguing the case and convincing us of our wrong. Why? Because He cares about the fellowship He sustains with His children. He knows that sin breaks off that fellowship. He wants fellowship to remain intact or, where conviction is necessary, to be restored. That is why He sends counselors as modern-day Nathans to modern-day Davids.

No process of change that ignores a counselee's relationship to God can succeed, no matter what gimmicks are used to get what the counselee wants. When a counselor attempts to change a counselee's behavior without first seeking change in his relationship with God, the result is merely outward, pharisaical behavior, just as displeasing to God as the original selfish behavior.

There is need for a full biblical study of the place of conviction in counseling. To the best of my knowledge, such a study does not yet exist. My sincere hope is that someone will produce one in the near future.

Assignment

In a case that you will be prepared to relate in class, show concretely how bringing a counselee to conviction of sin demonstrates God's loving care over him.

12

What Is Conviction?

The English word *conviction* is commonly used in three ways:

1. As in the phrase "a strong conviction," meaning a personal belief, or perhaps better, an *assured* personal belief.
2. As in the phrase "under conviction," meaning an uncomfortable sense of guilt before God or others. Used this way, the word usually implies that one has not yet repented of his sin and changed his wrong attitudes or behavior (though, of course, he may presently do so).
3. As in the sentence, "He was convicted of a crime." Here the word has an objective, legal force.

In which sense or senses is the biblical word used? Does *elegchos*, the term used in II Timothy 3:16, or the corresponding verb *elegcho* approximate any of the modern English uses?

In the previous chapter I hinted at the answer to that question when I spoke of the concern and the love God has for His children. You will remember that I said conviction, as a part of the process of divine change, is an evidence of God's care. I noted also that it has to do with the fellowship He and His children sustain toward one another. But I did not show the biblical basis for such notions. Let us investigate further.

Revelation 3:19, addressing the church at Laodicea, reads,

> "I convict and discipline those about whom I care; so be zealous and repent."

These words were written to the lukewarm church that Jesus, using a very bold figure of speech, said made Him sick enough to vomit (v. 16). It was the church that had said, "I am rich . . . I have become rich and have need of nothing" (v. 17). Because all seemed well outwardly, that congregation thought it was self-sufficient. Having "need of nothing," it saw no need for change. In short, it lacked conviction of sin. Jesus, however, warned its members that, in spite of their seeming well-being, they were, in His sight, "miserable and pitiable and poor and blind and naked." And Jesus urged,

> "I counsel you to buy from Me gold refined by fire that you may be rich, and white clothing that you may put on to cover your shameful nakedness, and eye-salve to anoint your eyes that you may see" (v. 18).

To those commands He then added the assurance, "I convict and discipline those about whom I care" (v. 19).

What can we learn from those gracious words? Among other things, we see that the risen Christ counsels the members of His church who are in need of change. Conviction of sin is part of that process. We discover also that the Laodicean church thought it needed no change, as if to say, "We've got it made." There surely would have been those who would have piously said, "Of course we are growing every day; we need to grow much more." But few would have acknowledged that great changes, resulting from repentance from sin, were necessary. That is why they needed to be convicted by the Savior Who cared. Change growing out of anything less than such conviction and disciplined correction is always insufficient.

Jesus explained that He convicts His people because He cares. He does not convict in order to punish or get even. The verb used in verse 19 is *phileo*, which means "to be friendly toward, to care for." The members of the Laodicean church had grown cold and haughty and had virtually locked Christ out of their church. He was standing outside knocking. Fellowship with the Lord had been broken (cf. Isa. 59:1, 2). When He urged them to open the door so that He might enter and dine with them, He was describing their need for restored fellowship with Him.[1]

What is the conviction of which Jesus spoke and what effect should it have had? The conviction of the church at Laodicea is said to be a *fait accompli*. Jesus is described as bringing about conviction by the words of the letter itself. The conviction did not depend on their response; they were not told to "come under conviction." What they were to do, in light of the conviction, was to be zealous (i.e., break out of their sinful complacency) and repent. Jesus Himself was doing the convicting. But because conviction can have unpleasant effects such as guilt feelings, He wanted them to know that He was acting out of love and concern for them.

The conviction of which Jesus spoke was not in the sense of "being under conviction" or of holding a strong personal belief, but in the sense of prosecuting His case against them. The word here has an objective sense, meaning "to so

1. This passage is wrongly used of unbelievers coming to faith in Christ; it has to do with believers who have by their sin shut Christ out of their lives.

prosecute a case against another that he is convicted of the crime of which he is accused." Such conviction is proving someone guilty. This objective conviction may lead to the subjective sense (of inducing a realization of guilt, though not always). Although their sin had been clearly exposed, the Laodiceans had yet to respond in repentance. The conviction of guilt may be apparent to all but the one who needs to repent.

Concerning the word *elegcho*, "to convict," Kittel says, "It means to show someone his sin and to summon him to repentance." Trench, in his *Synonyms*, distinguishes between *epitimao* and *elegcho*. The former is a rebuke that may or may not result in conviction; the latter always is successful. He says that in "juristic Greek *elegcho* is not merely to reply but to refute an opponent." Further, he writes,

> . . . *elegcho* implies not merely the charge, but the truth of the charge, and further the manifestation of the truth of the charge; nay more than all this, very often also the acknowledgement, if not outward, yet inward, of its truth on the part of the accused. . . .[2]

Notice two things in Trench's definition: (1) He says that where conviction occurs the charge is sustained: the truth of the charge is "manifested" to someone, though not necessarily to the one charged and convicted. A legal conviction may take place that is based upon false but seemingly compelling evidence, so that others are convinced of one's guilt and convict him of a crime. Yet the convicted one may protest the rightfulness of the conviction. (2) Trench, however, sees that as the exception to the rule. He thinks that, more often than not, the one who is convicted objectively (i.e., by others) is also convicted subjectively (i.e., by him-

2. Richard Chenevix Trench, *Synonyms of the New Testament* (Grand Rapids: Wm. B. Eerdmans, 1948), pp. 13-15.

self in his own heart) whether he admits so or not.

That seems precisely to be what we find in the New Testament usage of the term. Certainly those weak modern translations of *elegcho*, "rebuke" and "reprove," do not come anywhere near the real meaning. A rebuke or reproof may or may not be effective. A conviction, on the other hand, is always effective in convincing *someone*. When one is convicted, therefore, he is declared guilty of the crime of which he was accused—by the court, by himself, or by both. And, as Trench says, it is usually by both.

It is possible to acknowledge guilt inwardly or outwardly without repenting of it or changing one's ways. But there can be no repentance without acknowledging guilt. Until one is convinced of his wrongdoing, he cannot repent. The New Testament word for "repentance" is *metanoia*, which means, "a rethinking, a change of mind." Without an inner conviction of error and sin there is no reason for rethinking. And without conviction there is no reason to expect a change of behavior.

Conviction, then, is proving that charges made against someone are true. And, as Trench says, this usually leads to a subjective judgment as well as an objective one.

Let us now consider John 16:8-15, the classic passage on the coming of the Holy Spirit and His convicting ministry toward the world. The background of that passage is significant. In the last part of the fifteenth chapter and in the opening part of the sixteenth, among other things, Jesus was talking about the court trials that the apostles-to-be would experience. He assured them that the Spirit would directly give them the words to testify on such occasions and that the world that "hates" and "persecutes" (John 15:18, 20) would itself be convicted by that Spirit through the apostles' testimony to the truth. Here are some of the operative words:

"If I don't go away, the Advocate[3] certainly won't come
to you; but if I go, I will send Him to you. And when He
comes, He will convict [*elegcho*] the world about sin,
about righteousness and about judgment:
    about sin—because they don't believe in Me, about
    righteousness—because I am going to My Father and
    you won't see Me any more, and about judgment—
    because this world's ruler has been judged.
I still have much to tell you that you aren't able to bear
now, but when the Spirit of truth comes, He will guide
you into all truth. . . ."

The Holy Spirit is called the Advocate (*parakletos*). This
word is used of one who stands beside in order to assist as a
lawyer. He is a counselor-at-law. Plummer says the *parakletos* is "one summoned to the side . . . to aid in a court of
justice," and the conviction in which he is engaged may
bring salvation or condemnation.[4] In this passage, He
is represented as the One Who supplies all the wisdom,
knowledge, and speaking skills the apostles will need in
order to defend the truth and successfully make their case
about Christ when they are dragged before the rulers of
synagogs, before kings and governors and put on trial.
Through the apostles' proclamation of the Spirit's Word,
the world would be convicted. Tables would be turned, as
rulers' mouths would be stopped, and worldly prosecutors
would find *themselves* prosecuted—and convicted.

There are other passages that add to that very point:

"But when they deliver you up, don't worry about what
you will say or how you will say it, because what you
must say will be given to you in that hour. You aren't the
ones who will be speaking, but the Spirit of My Father
speaking in you" (Matt. 10:19-20).

3. Better than *Comforter* or *Counselor* (although *Counselor*, as counselor-
at-law, fits *exactly*).
4. A. Plummer, *The Cambridge Bible* (Cambridge, 1899), p. 279.

"Now when they arrest you and bring you to trial, don't worry beforehand about what you will say. Rather, say whatever is given to you in that hour (it won't be you speaking, but the Holy Spirit" (Mark 13:11).

". . . don't worry about what you will say in defense or how to do so, because the Holy Spirit will teach you in that very hour what you ought to say" (Luke 12:11, 12).

"Get it settled in your hearts not to practice your defense beforehand because I will give you words and wisdom that none of your opponents will be able to withstand or contradict"[5] (Luke 21:14, 15).

"The Holy Spirit . . . will teach you everything and remind you of everything that I told you"John 14:26).

But what of the threefold conviction by the Spirit through the Word preached during the trials? What does it mean?

The meaning of the words is not at first apparent. But in each case the meaning must inhere in the explanations given for each point. Though interpretations of these words differ, the meaning seems to be as follows: The Holy Spirit will convict the world's rulers of their sin of not believing in Jesus Christ as Savior. It will be shown that they have no personal integrity behind their unbelief; the only basis for such unbelief is willful sin. Through the apostles the Holy Spirit will also make out a case that Christ's resurrection and ascension, by which He returned to the Father, demonstrate conclusively His righteousness and truthfulness. The resurrection authenticates and vindicates Him before the world. The Holy Spirit, moreover, will convict the world's persecuting authorities that in the cross Satan has been judged and dethroned as the prince of this world, a position he had usurped in the first place. They will be convicted of

5. Here especially the powerful, successful nature of the Holy Spirit's convicting words through them is etched out.

their sinful attack on Christ, their feeble arguments in the face of the testimony of His resurrection and ascension, and the futility of their position; they follow a defeated leader as subjects of a falling kingdom.

In all of this we see at work the same dynamic observed before: conviction is brought about by the ministry of the Word. The Spirit does not *directly* convict men. He guided the apostles into all truth and instructed them about what to say and how to say it. It may be said that the Spirit convicts and that the Word convicts, as does the one ministering God's Word in His Name. All three elements are operative.

To summarize, we have seen that *conviction* means bringing facts to bear upon a case so as to prove someone guilty of a sin. Conviction in the New Testament is used primarily, if not exclusively, in this legal, objective sense. This must be kept in mind throughout the remaining chapters on this all-important step.

Assignment

In a major paper, trace the use of the word *conviction* through the New Testament, commenting, in particular, on its objective or subjective uses.

13

Conviction and Data Gathering

Because I have thoroughly discussed data gathering in *The Christian Counselor's Manual*, I shall not attempt to outline the advantages, process, or techniques of data gathering here. In this chapter my concern is to relate data gathering to change, specifically conviction in change.

There is one reason why data gathering is essential to convicting a counselee: unless the counselor knows the facts—enough facts to fully understand the counseling situation—he cannot call for repentance with the assurance he needs. If Nathan did not have the data, he could not have said to David, "You are the man!"

Since you do not have divine revelation about another's heart or absolute knowledge about what has transpired in his life, you will not always possess the same assurance Nathan had (see II Sam. 12:1, 7ff.). But the more accurate your data and the more you put these data into proper perspective, the more assurance you will have and the more effective your counseling will be. That is why data gathering is such an important part of the second step in the process of change.

Data alone, however, will not bring conviction. The data

you gather must be (1) interrelated, (2) interpreted according to biblical categories, and (3) used to reach biblical conclusions stated in biblical terms.

Expressing conclusions in biblical terminology is important. Few are likely to be convicted by conclusions such as, "Well, your problem seems to be neurosis," or, "At the bottom of these difficulties is a basic emotional problem," or, "You are suffering from a bad case of low self-esteem." None of these unbiblical terms (which grow out of unbiblical constructs) describes sinful behavior or attitudes over which one should repent. Neither "neurosis" nor "emotional problems" nor "low self-esteem" is a cause for conviction. How could you make out a case against one for having "emotional" difficulties? The very thought is absurd.[1]

Sin is disobedience to the law of God. It is an offense against one's Creator. Whenever a person does what God has forbidden or fails to do what He has commanded, he sins. The legal word *conviction* was chosen by the biblical writers because it speaks of bringing a case against a lawbreaker. And that is precisely what we are whenever we sin—lawbreakers.[2] In the analysis of a counselee's problems, any construct or terminology that denies or minimizes lawbreaking will fail to bring conviction to the counselee.

Again, one cannot be kinder than God. As Menninger has noted in his book, *Whatever Became of Sin?* all sorts of people carry loads of guilt around because modern constructs of human problems do not allow for the concept of sin and thus do not allow for forgiveness. The cruelest thing a counselor can do is to consign a guilty person to a state of

1. Of course, psychological jargon and constructs have been designed, in part, to eliminate a sense of guilt in the counselee.
2. "Whoever is committing sin also is breaking the law; indeed, sin is lawlessness" (I John 3:4).

nonforgiveness by eliminating the biblical constructs of lawbreaking and sin. Forgiveness is exactly what the person needs.

Reaching the conclusion that a counselee has sinned, the counselor can point to forgiveness in Christ through His substitutionary, penal, and sacrificial death on the cross. I shall say more about this later, but here let me emphasize that the kindest move on the part of any counselor is to label what is truly sin "sin." There is forgiveness for *sin*, not for "neurosis" or an "emotional problem"! There is really no solution to problems described by labels that mask the very root of those problems.[3]

Consider a case: Suppose the data you are gathering from a counselee is couched in the jargon of the psychologists, and your notes include the following two entries:

"John claims his problem is rejection."
"He says he has a bad self-image as the result of others' putting him down."

How could you do anything with that? First of all, it is obvious that there are no biblical categories for "problems of rejection" and "bad self-images." So, in your attempt to help John you will not be able to match these statements with any biblical categories; the problem, as stated, precludes a biblical solution. Even before attempting to offer a solution, you will be stymied in that you cannot bring the counselee to conviction. As long as problems are addressed in terms of "rejection" or "bad self-images," no biblical case can be made against them as sins. Indeed, such labels imply a case against others, who have made John the victim of their sins when in fact John is a violator of God's law.

Now, of course, we do not want to accuse people of

3. For more on this subject I refer you to my book, *The Language of Counseling and the Christian Counselor's Wordbook* (Grand Rapids: Zondervan Publishing House, 1986).

sinning who have not sinned; that is what Job's counselors did. And the disciples were prepared to do the same concerning the blind man in John 9. But in this book I am not dealing with situations in which one bears no responsibility for his plight. We are presupposing, therefore, that John's problems are, at least in part, self-generated. Yet, because of the modern tendency to shift blame onto others or one's circumstances, the data you receive from counselees and others will often be shaped by the victim theme.

When you get data in that form, you must work at re-shaping it into a more biblical form both for yourself and for the counselee. Only then will you find the fit between data and biblical principle necessary to reaching a biblical solution.

Consider the following:

"I guess I act the way I do because my parents rejected me."

"What happened, John, is that you learned to handle wrongdoing toward yourself in a sinful way. Just what sorts of things did you do when you thought you were being rejected? Let's see if we can get a biblical handle on precisely how you respond to such treatment so that we can describe in exact biblical terms the response pattern you have been following since childhood. Then, and only then, can we bring the right biblical solution to it."

Perhaps later in the session something like this would be heard:

"I have a rotten self-image, you see; people have always been putting me down."

"In other words, you are saying that you accepted false-hood as truth. Instead of refusing to do so, you went right along with these 'put downs,' began to think of yourself in inaccurate ways, and allowed your life to be shaped by these thoughts. To believe lies about yourself is sin. Romans 12:3b requires you to make a 'sober judgment' about yourself. Of course, as a child, coming into the world with a sinful, corrupted nature, you would naturally do such things. But as a Christian and an adult, you must no longer believe these lies. Then again, we shall have to study the facts carefully to see if some of the things others have said are not lies after all. In that case, it may be that we are also facing a bit of resentment or some self-deceit as well."

Describing the problem as a sinful response pattern (which eventually will be identified and stated in biblical terms) puts the responsibility where it belongs—on John's shoulders. He himself has caused this problem, and he must be convicted. He must not be allowed to blame others for his condition. If John's problem were caused by others in his past, he might be stuck with it for life. After all, what's done is done. On the other hand, if a habitual, sinful response can be identified, such as John's accepting lies as truth or harboring resentment or engaging in self-deceit, such a sinful response can be mercifully forgiven and biblically changed.

Perhaps these all-too-typical examples demonstrate the importance of gathering and shaping the data in biblical terms. Otherwise, there will be no way to bridge the gap between identifying the infringement of God's law (spelled out in step one) and bringing about "correction" (step three), along with "disciplined training in righteousness" (step four). Just as repentance (step three) is a prerequisite for retraining in the way of righteousness (step four), there can be no repentance from sin without conviction for law-breaking (step two). People simply don't repent over being wronged by others.

Perhaps you are wondering, "But will the counselee accept your reshaping and renaming of the data?" That is a

good question, the full answer to which must wait until I
discuss the use of the Scriptures in conviction. But here let
me salute you for recognizing that sometimes you must
discuss the point at length with the counselee in order to
convict and convince him. And let me assure you, while the
matter is still fresh in your mind, that the best way to
convince counselees of their need to look at matters differently is to show them that they are not analyzing the problem biblically. This can best be done by noting (1) that the
Bible does not entertain the categories and terminology the
counselee is using, and (2) that in scriptural cases similar to
his, the Bible describes his kind of behavior or attitudes as
sin.

The key point to stress is that no matter how others treat a
person, he must respond biblically (see Rom. 12:14, 17-21 to
make this point). Remember that when men spat on Christ,
He didn't handle their sin sinfully.[4]

So, you see that conviction and data gathering are in-
separably related. How one gathers data and the terminology he uses to state it may make all the difference in counseling. Indeed, it may determine whether counseling will
proceed toward the other two steps or whether it will be
short-circuited at step two.

Assignment

Select a case from *The Christian Counselor's Casebook*, and
in a three-page paper show how data must be gathered and
shaped into biblical form in order to solve the case.

---

4. Nor did He develop a "rotten self-image" or become "neurotic."

14

The Use of the Scriptures in Conviction

I have made a point of saying that the Spirit uses the Scriptures to bring about sanctifying change in regenerate people. If that is so, and if, as II Timothy 3 indicates, the Scriptures are "useful" for convicting of sin, then we must know how to use the Scriptures in convicting counselees.

The role of the Scriptures in bringing about conviction is commonly ignored in counseling books. We are readily told of the comforting and guiding power of the Scriptures, and that is good; but what about their convicting power? Because the Scriptures do convict, you must deliberatively use them for that purpose. That means learning how to use them skillfully.

The deliberate, skillful use of the Scriptures in bringing conviction of sin to counselees involves at least the following factors:

1. Knowledge of what Scripture portions to use for what specific convicting purposes.
2. The ability to explain thoroughly any and all portions used.
3. Skill in showing counselees how the Holy Spirit in-

tended to convict him of sin through a given passage. Let me take up these three factors in order.

In three other books I have stressed the need for knowing key passages of Scripture: in *The Use of the Scriptures in Counseling*, in *The Christian Counselor's New Testament*, and especially in *What to Do on Thursday* (where I have set forth a program for developing such knowledge).[1] All three books contain lists of key passages. Rather than duplicate available material here, let me make one other suggestion: whenever you have successfully used a passage of Scripture to convict a counselee, make a note of the passage and how you used it. The list of passages in the *Christian Counselor's New Testament* (pp. 743ff.) provides space for recording such data. Or you may want to develop your own list of passages in some convenient form for reference during counseling. You will find yourself turning to it time and again.

Let's take an example. You have been counseling with Ted, a Christian, who tells you of his "overwhelming desire" to fondle little girls. He claims that he cannot help it and that he has tried to stop, but this "desire, like a power greater than myself," as he puts it, just takes over before he realizes what he has done. And he maintains self-righteously the attitude that "since I can't help myself, it's not my fault."

Familiar with the words of Peter 4:1, 2, you read them to him:

Since Christ has suffered in the flesh, arm yourselves with that thought, because whoever has suffered in the flesh has come to a parting of the ways with sin. As a result, it is now possible to live the remainder of your time in the flesh no longer following human desires, but following the will of God.

1. Available from Presbyterian and Reformed Publishing Company, Phillipsburg, N.J.

Peter's words, when pressed, explained, and applied to Ted's situation, put an end to his excuse making, convict him of sin, and bring him to repentance, including an eagerness to change. You would, therefore, do well to make a note of that passage, recording it this way:

I Peter 4:1, 2: use to counter claim that desire is uncontrollable or overwhelming.

Such a notation, brief and to the point, is just what you may need six months from now to jog your memory. If you are including it in a list of items, alphabetically arranged, you might want to enter it under the heading "Desire."

But what if quoting the verse, as pertinent as it is, does not bring immediate conviction to the counselee? What if he protests, or argues that he is an exception? You may need to explain more fully the passage in I Peter 4 and show how the Holy Spirit intended it to apply to Ted's situation:

Ted: "But Pastor, you don't understand. I have a sort of special problem. This is an overwhelming desire that just takes over. I don't want it to; it just does."

Pastor: "Yes, I know your desire can be strong, especially when you have submitted to it for years. The Scriptures clearly indicate that one can become a slave to his desires: 'At one time we too were foolish, disobedient, and enslaved to various desires and pleasures. . . . but . . .' (Titus 3:3, 4[a]).[2] Notice the 'but.' What Paul is saying to Titus—that in Christ the Christian has been emancipated from such slavery—Peter likewise is saying to you: through Christ's death you have been freed from the overwhelming power of sin. Christ has made it possible for you to turn away from enslaving desires and to do His will. You must believe that and come to see that continued indulgence in your sinful

2. This is another passage to list under "desire" with the notation: "desire enslaves," or "freedom from slavery of desire."

desires can in no way be justified. Sanctification takes place only in faith (Gal. 3:2-4). Perhaps you have tried to quit and failed. There are good reasons for failure other than saying that your case is an exception. God does not lie. He says it is now possible to free yourself from this sinful desire and the practices that it entails. You must repent of that sin and call on Him to forgive you and give you the knowledge and power to refrain from it in the future. Once you do that, we will examine in detail why you are failing and what you must do instead to succeed.[3] But first you must acknowledge that your behavior cannot be excused, that it is sin. That's where we must begin."

In the exchange above, in which the pastor must do much explaining, you will notice that he challenges Ted's rationalization, rather than accept it. Contrary to Ted's alibis, the passage says it is possible to resist sin. Ted and the Holy Spirit are at odds, and the pastor makes that clear (perhaps even in so many words). The Holy Spirit does not hold out false hope. Whatever promises He makes, He keeps.

If, however, that tack fails to bring conviction, the counselor may need to make a point of the purpose (*telos*) of the passage:

"Ted, why do you think the Holy Spirit put these words here? There are many Christians just like you who have given up because they have failed in the past. He wants to assure them that there is hope. And He certainly intended to remove any excuses from those who sinfully persist in evil practices."

After such explanations, and the specific application of the intention of the passage to Ted and his situation, the

3. Verse 1 will have something to say about the problem. If he doesn't think change is possible through Christ's victory over sin, it won't be possible for him to "arm himself" with thoughts and attitudes necessary to meet and withstand the attacks of sinful desires.

counselor will often find that the Word has done its work; the Spirit has used it to bring about conviction. But, in some cases, resistance will continue:

"No, you don't understand. My case is different. . . ." In such an event, the pastor may need to drive home the point of I Corinthians 10:13 that there are no exceptions.[4]

Of course, there will be times when resistance continues, in spite of what you do. The counselor may wait a week or so to see if the Spirit will yet use the presentation of the Word that was given. It may be wise to send the counselee home with an assignment to read and pray over the passages the counselor has discussed with him. And the counselor will make it clear that counseling cannot continue until repentance takes place. Conviction must not be by-passed. If, at length, there is continued refusal to acknowledge sin and repent, the counselor may have to institute the process of church discipline, in which one or two others (and eventually the whole church, if necessary, must continue to bring relevant scriptural exhortation to bear upon the reluctant brother (see, especially, II Thess. 3:15[b]). Throughout, he must be confronted with the Word in order to be brought to conviction.

In the previous chapter I alluded to the parable Nathan used to convict David of his sin (II Sam. 12:13). Notice that David was convicted out of his own mouth. The same technique of bringing conviction can be found in II Samuel 14:1ff. and in I Kings 20:39ff. Counselors may occasionally wish to employ this tactic; so let us analyze the approach structurally.

It consists of (1) telling a parable involving a wrongdoing analogous to the counselee's sin, (2) eliciting the counselee's reaction against the wrongdoing in the parable, and

4. Another verse that can be used powerfully in cases where refusal persists is Prov. 13:15: "The way of the transgressor is hard."

(3) drawing the connection between what the counselee condemns and his own sin. Of course, the element of surprise is lessened by the counseling situation, but even so, the method still may be used effectively.

Let's see how:

> *Counselor:* "A man was given a traffic ticket for speeding and he paid the fine. Three days later the police came around to his house and hauled him off to jail, where he was locked up for seven days for the very same crime. Was that just?"
>
> *Fred:* "Of course not. You can't be held liable for a crime after you've already paid its penalty. It's a matter of simple justice."
>
> *Counselor:* "Well, you've done the same thing to your boy. He was punished in school for his cheating, and now you have punished him again at home for the very same offense. It's a case of simple *in*justice!"

The counselor might go on to show Fred that he should explain to his boy why punishing him a second time is unwarranted, and the counselor might also urge him instead to sit down and talk to the boy about the cheating in the light of what it means to Christ.[5] He may further encourage the father to help his son overcome his cheating, and his poor work or study habits, which occasioned the temptation to cheat.

Parables should not take the place of Scripture. They should be used, as in a sermon, to emphasize, clarify, or make memorable some truth or principle of Scripture that otherwise might not be received as readily.

While the points I have been making in this chapter are not particularly profound, they are important, especially

5. Punishment alone is not adequate. Eph. 6:4 requires both "nurture" (i.e., discipline that includes punishment when necessary) and "admonition" (i.e., "nouthetic confrontation" or counseling). Too often admonition is omitted.

since they are rarely mentioned. Having been alerted to their importance, you as a concerned counselor will be able to take it from here on your own. If you need more help, I direct your attention to *What to Do on Thursday*, in which, among other things, a six-month program for learning the location of critical biblical passages is set forth.

Assignment

1. Make a preliminary list of passages that would seem to be appropriate for bringing conviction to counselees in counseling.
2. Categorize these under headings, alphabetically listed.
3. Beside each make a brief, one-line notation about its use.
4. Hand in a photocopy of your work by _____.
   (date)

15

Supplementary Thoughts About Conviction

There are several items that, while not requiring separate chapters, ought to be discussed when we are thinking about conviction in counseling. I shall lump them together in this chapter, taking up each one, without any thought of logical order.

First, let me mention the problem of conviction and need. Since I have written elsewhere about the current tendency among counselors to speak of committing sin as meeting a "need," here it is important simply to warn you of the innumerable occasions on which such "needs" will have to be debated scripturally. If a counselee believes that his sinful behavior is somehow *necessary* and therefore excusable, you must set the record straight. No one needs to disobey Scripture. Unless you clearly differentiate *needs* from sinful desires (however strong), conviction will not take place.

Secondly, the emphasis here on conviction of sin runs counter to the on-coming avalanche of teaching in counseling that I predict for the future. I am not a prophet, and naturally I could be wrong. But given the way the church tends eclectically to follow the swinging pendulum of the world, it seems likely that the present wave of emotion-centered, irrational counseling will soon give way to a new intellectualism. Cognitive counseling of the variety set forth by the modern Stoic Albert Ellis, and in modified forms already mimicked by some Christian counselors, will be upon us before we know it. In such counseling, getting people's heads straight is the goal; we are told "if they think straight, they'll act right, and their attitudes will be proper too." Nonsense!

Every biblical counselor should be aware that there is a moral side to change. (In James, even doubt is treated from the moral rather than the intellectual perspective.) When, therefore, you are tempted to skip over conviction and correction, as if righteousness flows from intellectual change alone, remember this: the biblical process of change outlined by Paul has four, not two, steps. A man who merely gives assent to truth, who merely corrects the errors of his thinking without repenting of sin, when there is sin involved, does not change in God's way.

Thirdly, however, let me make it clear that conviction must not become a morbid, drawn-out exercise in introspection. The idea is not to make the counselee sweat it out. There are people in the church who have revived the notion of some Puritans that people must repent of their sins over long periods of time. No such thing is in view. The discussion should continue until the conviction has been carried out, no longer. When a counselee acknowledges that he has sinned, makes no excuses for his sin, is sorry and seeks God's forgiveness, counseling must move on. I am not denying that there may be great emotion connected with this process. That is all well and good so long as it is a genuine expression of sorrow. But never give the idea that emotionalism is the objective, something to be pretended. Some people do not readily express their emotions, even though their sorrow, grief, or pain is felt every bit as keenly as others. God does not ask us to tally the emotional responses that accompany conviction; He tells us to look for the fruit of repentance in a changed lifestyle. Moreover, if you detect the slightest hint of emotionalism as a meritorious activity, squelch it immediately. Even faith is not meritorious; all merit accredited to us is Christ's, not ours.

Fourthly, there are those whose consciences have been dulled, perhaps even "seared"[1] by lies, hypocrisy, and a failure to listen to truth. Such people must be confronted about that dullness itself and the scriptural need for change must be freshly pressed upon them. Sometimes, however, the only thing that restores life to the deadened nerve cells of a seared conscience is the threat or actual pursuit of church discipline. Some people must be "taught by discipline" (I Tim. 1:20). That is unfortunate, but for their sakes, as well as for the purity of the church and the Name of Christ, such persons must be excommunicated if all else fails.

Finally, it certainly takes some boldness to confront people about their sin. I recognize that. But in counseling, people have asked you to look closely into their lives, and they must expect you to do just that. To be a faithful servant of Christ, you must tell them what you find in them—even if that is not very complimentary. How do you do so? Look at the Epistles of Paul. Rarely is there a stinging word to his errant converts. Usually the ink on his pages was blotted with tears. He wrote plainly, but with no sense of superiority; with authority, yet always with meekness. In short, everything about his words indicates sorrow at his having

1. If "seared" means totally destroyed, as it might in I Tim. 4:2, where the concept is introduced and is applied to apostates, then the word may be inappropriate for describing the desensitization of a *believer's* conscience, which is always in part and never irremedial.

to write such things. Nevertheless, he never trimmed his sails (cf. his words to the Ephesian elders, Acts 20).

But there is another note that pervades the writings of the New Testament. It is the note of optimism. Nowhere do the writers give up on God's people—not even when they were forced to excommunicate some of them. Hope resounds on every convicting page. After all, that is the great fact about Christianity: we Christians believe in change. God is the God of change. He sent His Son to effect the basis for change, and His Spirit and His Word to bring it to pass. With such realities before us, we too as Christian counselors must never despair of any regenerate person, no matter how miserably he acquits himself. He who is in him is greater than he who is in the world. Nothing the devil has can compete with the Spirit. And where sin abounds, grace *far more* abounds (Rom. 5:20). Remember, He is able to do surpassingly more than you could ever ask or think!

Assignment

Choose one:
1. Study the wrong use of the word "need" in recent counseling books written by Christians and report on your findings.
2. Study boldness in ministry in the Bible and report on this study.
3. Exegete the passages having to do with "dullness" and with a "seared conscience," and report on your work.

PART IV

STEP THREE, CORRECTION

16

What Is Correction?

The Word of God wounds, but it also binds up; it cuts out the soul's cancer, and then it heals the soul (see Isa. 30:26). Conviction is the unpleasant task whereby the counselor brings a biblical case against a counselee for his sin. But if the counselor served simply as a prosecuting attorney, his job would be miserable and disheartening. He uses the Word not only to knock counselees prostrate before the holy God they have offended, but also to put them back on their feet.

That is the idea behind the Greek word *epanorthosis*, translated "correction" in II Timothy 3:16. It is the sense of "standing something up" or "making something to stand again." In modern Greek it has come to mean "redress, reparation, rectifying." But in New Testament times it had not altogether lost the pictorial idea behind it, if, indeed, it has today. So, the Word of God has the positive power of rectifying what has gone wrong. It is able to set straight what has been knocked off base or out of line.

Epanorthosis is used only here in the New Testament. But it is found frequently in the papyri with the meaning of "correction," as in the correction of papers (see Moulton and Milligan).

Whether the picture is of the Scriptures knocking one down and then picking him up, dusting him off, and setting him straight with God once again, or of the Bible straightening him up after sin has knocked him askew matters little. Both ideas are biblical, if not implied in the verse at hand.

When you consider that the Bible is concerned not only with exposing wrongs, but also with righting[1] them, you begin to get some idea about the vast ministering enterprise toward which God's Word is oriented. The Bible boldly claims to supply what is necessary to help one change any attitudes or behaviors out of accord with God's will. The Bible not only shows us God's will and convicts us of failure to follow it, but helps us to get out of the messes into which we fall when we don't obey. We must not limit its resources or scope.

In this third step we shall consider each of the elements in the process of correction and how the counselor brings them together in the life of the counselee.

An important modern concept that has grown from the relatively young science of cybernetics is the idea of feedback. Feedback of information allows a missile, a computer, or a person to make changes calculated to correct divergence from a desired course. Long before Norbert Wiener coined the word cybernetics (taken from the Greek term for "helmsman," or "pilot"), God was already directing His ministers to put people back on course by means of the Scriptures. In counseling, that is done as counselors pro-

---

1. "Righting" may be our closest English equivalent to *epanorthosis*.

vide feedback to show counselees where they have gone wrong and what corrections they must make.[2]

That is what we shall be studying in the third step of change as it is set forth in II Timothy 3.

2. Because a person rarely gets honest and accurate feedback from others, he often continues the same sinful course, self-deceived. Though it takes boldness, counselors must learn to become a source of full and truthful feedback, responding biblically to their counselees' behavior, expressed ideas, and attitudes. One of the most important functions performed by biblical counselors is giving counselees accurate readings on their lifestyles. As we have seen, these "readings" should always be phrased in biblical language in accordance with biblical categories.

Unlike people who are frank and honest only when speaking about someone behind his back (in violation of James 4:11), a Christian counselor must lovingly speak the truth to his counselee's face, in order to foster correction.

17

Correction and Repentance

Like conviction, *repentance* is a word rarely heard in counseling, even in supposedly Christian counseling circles. Yet the vital role of repentance as a biblical prerequisite to correcting a counselee's sin cannot be denied (cf. Rev. 2:5). The counselee who has sinned needs plainly to repent.

The English word *repent* is a virtual transliteration of a Latin word, which in turn is an exact translation of the Greek, *metanoia*. This New Testament word, like the Latin and English terms built on it, means "to rethink." Repentance is a rethinking of one's behavior, attitudes, and beliefs. It is coming to a different opinion or viewpoint, one so different that it calls for different thought patterns and a different lifestyle. There is nothing in the word *metanoia* about sorrow; indeed it does not speak of the emotions at all. That is not to say that true repentance will not lead to sorrow, but the word itself carries no such connotation.

The translation of another word, as "repentance," in the King James Version, has misled some to look for outward expressions of emotion as proof of genuine repentance. That word in its verbal form is *metamelomai*, meaning "to express regret, sorrow, remorse," as in the case of Judas' emotional experience after betraying the Lord (Matt. 27:3). Such sorrow does not involve repentance. In *metamelos* a person regrets his actions because of their consequences (usually to himself), not necessarily because they were wrong as sins against a holy God. In Hebrews 12:17, Esau is presented as having not been able to undo the circumstance brought about by his sin (he could not "repent," rectify, or correct the situation), in spite of his great emotional outbursts. His regret did not amount to repentance. According to II Corinthians 7:10, it is *"godly* sorrow" (or pain) that produces repentance (*metanoia*), which is never to be confused with ungodly sorrow or self-centered regret. Clearly, Esau's sorrow and Judas' regret did not lead to *metanoia,* because their concerns were not in harmony with what God required. They lacked "godly sorrow."

Repentance is more than regret, even godly regret. Although all true repentance involves regret for having offended God, that emotional side of the process is neither the sum total of repentance nor always manifest to others. In the Scriptures, the evidence of repentance is not regret, but "fruit" resulting from and appropriate to repentance. That is clear from the preaching of John, Christ, and the apostles.[1]

There is always the possibility that someone will hypocritically feign behavior and words that seem to evidence repentance. But that seldom lasts long. Since God alone knows the hearts of men (I Sam. 16:7), the counselor must look on the "outward appearance" alone. He has been called to make a functional, righteous judgment, based on fruit that should accompany repentance. That functional

1. See, for instance, Matt. 25:31ff.; 7:16ff.; Rev. 20:12, 14. Judgment, not salvation, is based on fruit (works), which is the evidence of salvation.

judgment has to do with how the church must relate or function in reference to someone, either *"as* a brother" or *"as* a heathen and a tax collector"—as repentant or not. The same distinction is implied in the words of James when he pointedly challenges those who talk a good game, but give no evidence of knowing how to play it: "Show me your faith without works and I will show you my faith by works" (James 2:18). That desire to see the fruit of repentance is one reason why the counselor requires "homework" (for details on this see *The Christian Counselor's Manual*).

So, repentance is a change of mind about one's beliefs, attitudes, and behavior that involves regret about sin and issues in a change of lifestyle as outward evidence of a desire to be different. It encompasses the following:

1. Confessing sin to God and to others (the outward expression of godly regret).
2. Seeking forgiveness (the first step taken to remedy the situation).
3. Forsaking the sinful way (the next remedial step).
4. Beginning an alternative way of life that is pleasing to God (the last corrective step).

Let me reemphasize that correction takes place by means of Scripture. The change of mind that leads to regretting and confessing sin, seeking forgiveness, and putting on a new biblical lifestyle cannot be achieved by the counselor and the counselee on their own. It is something the Spirit brings about through the Word. Because the Spirit works through the Bible, the writing of which He Himself superintended over many years, the counselor must not attempt to correct a counselee's lifestyle apart from the Bible. To do so is to encourage hypocrisy, instead of correction flowing from a changed heart.

When the Spirit applies the Bible to the repentant minds of His regenerate people, the fruit of the Spirit is cultivated and grows. Such concrete deeds are what John the Baptist looked for in the lives of his listeners:

"Bear fruits that are appropriate to repentance, and don't begin saying to yourselves, 'We have Abraham as our father.' . . . Whoever has two coats must share with the one who doesn't have any, and whoever has food must do likewise" (Luke 3:8, 11; cf. Gal. 5:22).

The acts described by John are manifestations of "kindness and goodness," i.e., good deeds and kind actions toward others, and concrete expressions of "love." More specifically, John told tax collectors and soldiers that repentance will affect their everyday jobs:

"Don't collect any more than you are supposed to. . . . Don't extort money by intimidating or by false accusation, and be satisfied with your pay" (Luke 3:13, 14).

John struck hard at the besetting sins of each group. In such prohibitions, as in all of God's negative commandments, the corresponding positive fruit of the Spirit is equally required. Thus John commanded not only the *abandonment* of sinful practices, but also the *adoption* of action that is the fruit of love toward one's neighbor. In other words, John specifically demanded the *correction* of sinful ways in the lives of professedly repentant persons. That is precisely what biblical counselors must do today. They must not stop at giving general suggestions.

Let's consider a case in point. Bill, a professed Christian, is a homosexual.[2] He claims to be concerned about what he is doing and has asked for help. To help him you first must

2. While biblical counselors cannot accept everything found in it (especially the adoption of Mowrer's Integrity Therapy groups) John W. Drakeford's book, *A Christian View of Homosexuality* (Nashville: Broadman Press, 1977), is in many ways very helpful and informative. Every counselor should be acquainted with it.

convict him of his sin. There can be no acceptable change of life without a corresponding change of heart. God wants truly repentant people. So, the first thing is to make out a solid, convincing, biblical case against homosexuality. Bill's expressed concern may be only about the consequences of his lifestyle to himself. There may be regret but no repentance, no change of mind of the sort that God requires. When that "change of mind" takes place, and Bill sees homosexuality not just as a dangerously unhealthy way of life, but as sin against God and his neighbor and is willing to confess it as such, forsake it in thought and deed, and begin a new way of life pleasing to God, he will be on his way toward making the change that God requires of him.

Along with seeking God's forgiveness, Bill may also need to seek the forgiveness of others, such as his wife or parents. He then must forsake all alliances to those with whom he has been committing homosexual acts. Abandoning such connections indicates the early growth of outward fruit appropriate to repentance. Likewise, according to I Corinthians 15:33, he must rid himself of every influence that might lead him back into homosexuality. That is the idea behind the doctrine of radical amputation, in which Jesus ordered us to eliminate the right hand, foot, or eye if it presents a temptation to sin (Matt. 5:29; 18:8ff.; Mark 9:42-48). The fourth step, disciplined training in righteousness—the putting on of an entirely different way of thinking and living—is also necessary, but we have not yet reached that point.

Correction is the pivotal point of change, in which the transfer of thought and life from non-biblical to biblical ways begins. The Bible is useful to effect this transfer from erroneous thought about God, others, and oneself, and from the sinful living that accompanies it, to truth and holiness. Correction is God picking us up, brushing us off, turning us around, and giving us a shove in the right direction, all, of course, by the Scriptures ministered in the power of the Spirit.

Assignment

Study the repentance of *Christians* in the New Testament. Be prepared to discuss your findings in class.

18

Confession of Sin and Forgiveness

In Proverbs 28:13 we read, "He who conceals his transgressions will not prosper, but he who confesses and forsakes them will receive mercy."

In this chapter, we shall look at confession and the forgiveness of sin; in the next, at forsaking sin. And the place to begin, once again, is with the words involved. Word study is of great importance when it comes to pivotal terms like *confession*, *correction*, and *repentance*. Understanding the meaning and usage of the words in question takes one beyond mere conjecture about what God is saying.[1]

Proverbs 28:13 contains the word *yadah*, the standard Old Testament term for confession. The idea behind the word is "to throw or to cast." It is used of casting lots and counting votes and has come to mean "to recount or tell one's story."

---

1. Too much conjecture about or misunderstanding of biblical concepts is set forth as fact in the books on Christian counseling, especially by authors who are fond of integration and whose backgrounds are in psychology rather than in biblical exegesis.

It relates to telling the facts about something, thus "to confess, or make known some sin."[2]

The New Testament term *homologeo*, or in the more intensive form *exomologeo*, means "to say (or 'speak out') the same thing." In the light of what we have seen already, it means that when the case is made against a counselee (he has been convicted of the crime of which he was accused), he openly agrees with the pronouncement that he is guilty. Throughout the papyri one runs across the verbal form of this word (*homologeo*) in contracts in which it is regularly translated, "I agree to" or "I acknowledge that." The word obviously had an official or at least quasi-official usage, therefore, in which one publicly acknowledged or agreed to something. That too is the idea in the New Testament. *Homologia* cannot be used to denote a mere private, subjective acknowledgment of something; it always has an objective character about it in which the acknowledgment is made *to someone else*. In Christian counseling, the someone else is first God, then, if need be, any other who has been wronged.

This willingness to acknowledge one's guilt, to agree with the conviction, is uppermost in the idea of confession. When coupled with the Old Testament notion of telling or recounting what has taken place (or even of "pointing out" what one has done), it brings the full biblical concept to the fore. Confession is the act of acknowledging one's guilt by telling another that one has committed the wrong of which he has been accused. Of course, one may take the initiative and accuse and convict himself of the sin all in the same act. Thus confession can also become an act of self-conviction.

---

2. Some think that the idea of casting the hand in a certain direction, thus indicating or pointing to something (e.g., pointing out one's sin), is the figure that lies behind the word.

Either way, agreeing to certain stated charges is the basic notion in confession.

The Purpose of Confession

Confession is not a psychological ploy to "get a sense of guilt off one's chest." It is a sinner's acknowledgment of his guilt against another in order to seek his forgiveness and achieve reconciliation. Because it recounts or points out the facts, confession is not general ("sorry I wronged you") but specific ("I stole $243.02 from you").[3] And to the specific acknowledgment of one's guilt is added the words, "Will you forgive me?" A mere apology ("I'm sorry") does not achieve reconciliation because it does not request forgiveness, which alone can close the matter. In response to an apology (the world's substitute for seeking biblical forgiveness) the offended party does not have to promise to put the matter behind him. A request for forgiveness, however, elicits a promise from the offended party to remember the offense no more and thus not raise it to him, to others, or to himself. The matter is closed. If the offended party refuses to grant that request, he, himself, becomes subject to the church discipline outlined in Matthew 18:15ff., which is designed to lead to forgiveness and reconciliation.

So, confession is a critical element in the process of change. Without it, there can be no forgiveness and reconciliation. If the counselor wishes to help people build a relationship with God or others, he must first clear away the rubble of the past to make room for an adequate foundation.

A failure to deal adequately with the past is the downfall of most counseling. If the people who campaign for un-

3. On this point, see Wescott on I John 1:9.

conditional "acceptance" have their way, counselors will accept counselees nonjudgmentally, looking only on the positive side. Such an approach implicitly condones the very sin and guilt of which it should dispose. If the Freudians, and those swayed by Freudian views, have their way, catharsis will preempt confession as the way to spell relief from the pressure of guilt. If others prevail, they will stress the need to deal with offenses toward men, but not toward God.[4] Which leads us to our next consideration.

God Forgives Sin

All sin, as David made clear, is against God. Even more important than seeking the forgiveness of others we have wronged is seeking forgiveness from God. Short of that, even the forgiveness we seek from others will be inadequate. When a man steals, he breaks one of God's commandments (Exod. 20:15). Any such violation of the law of God[5] requires seeking God's forgiveness.

God has told His children,

> If we confess our sins, He is faithful and righteous so that He may forgive our sins and cleanse us from all unrighteousness (I John 1:9).

That is a gracious promise. It means that, because of the shed blood of the Lord Jesus Christ, not only does God, the Judge, reckon our debt of sin paid and remit our sins, but God, the Holy One, looks on us in Christ as perfect—perfectly *clean* of all unrighteousness. No psychology or psy-

---

4. E.g., Mowrer's Integrity Therapy.

5. Sin is defined as such by the law (Rom. 7:7), not by the fact that others are hurt or alienated by our actions. Some today, even in so-called evangelical circles, define sin in terms of its horizontal effects rather than this vertical dimension.

chologist can offer anything like that. The stains of sin linger where there is no sacrificial blood to cleanse them. The guilt of sin remains where there is no judge to pronounce one acquitted because of the penal death of Christ. Freud, Rogers, Skinner, and others can offer no sacrifice, no substitute, no advocate with the Father! They therefore have no solution to the problem of sin. All they can do is mask guilt, or ignore it.

God is in the business of forgiving sin. How foolish to turn to someone else for the solution to a sin problem he is not even willing to recognize as sin! Yet, that is what millions of people do every day, not realizing themselves that they have a sin problem, which can be solved by none other than the Lord Jesus Christ. All the sadder that many so-called Christian counselors fail to call for repentance, confession of sins, and the seeking of forgiveness both from God and from man.

Assignment

Write a brief sketch of a counseling dialog in which the counselor is explaining to the counselee the need for confession. Picture the counselee merely wanting relief from the sense of guilt that he carries, while not wanting to confess his sin to anyone.[6] In the dialog show how the counselor might help him to move toward a more biblical position.

6. He may not even fully recognize that his offense is sin; perhaps because others have given it a psychological label, he is confused about the matter.

19

Forsaking Sin

Let us turn again to Proverbs 28:13 and look at the last part of the verse:

> He who conceals his transgressions will not prosper, but he who confesses and forsakes them will receive mercy.

The failure evident in most counseling results largely from failure to heed the words of this Proverb. God will not bless counseling that overlooks, excuses, condones, or "conceals" sin, which should be openly confessed to God and to others who have been wronged. Neither the counselor who propounds some other solution to sin nor the counselee who follows that "solution" will prosper, or "succeed."[1] One must not expect success when God has promised failure. But in spite of the clear words of Proverbs 28:13, people pursue paths that God has blocked. No wonder there is much failure.

---

1. *Tsaleach*, the Hebrew word, means "to go through," denoting the ability to penetrate all barriers and reach one's goals. No one, however, can pass through where God bars his way.

God calls us to *forsake* sin, which, according to the Hebrew word, means "to let go" of it. The person who, wit-
tingly or unwittingly, holds on to sin cannot expect the
blessing of God. God will not step aside and allow someone
to prosper toward his goals until he lets go of the sin to
which he is clinging.

"Letting go of" or "forsaking" sin is the same as "putting
off" sin, as the New Testament writers express it. It is half of
the two-factored process of putting off old, sinful patterns
of life and putting on new ones. Because step four treats the
positive side of the process, here I shall deal only with the
negative side, putting off.

Putting off sin is abandoning, quitting, forsaking, or letting go of sin. It includes the following:

1. A willingness to deny or say no (as Christ puts it) to
   selfish desires, either sinful in themselves or sinful as
   taking priority above Christ and His kingdom.
2. An actual breaking with the past practice, situation,
   or persons involved in the sin.
3. Setting up a structure that will make it difficult to fall
   into the same sin again.

The second and third elements in forsaking sin involve
what I have already spoken of as radical amputation. In
radical amputation—eliminating the right (i.e., most important) foot, hand, or eye, if necessary—one does two
things:

1. He eliminates anything, anyone, any influence, or
   any situation that may be a stumbling block to holy
   obedience to God's Word.
2. He makes it very difficult to sin unconsciously or
   habitually; sin would take a much more deliberate
   effort, given the figurative removal of one's sin-
   prone foot, hand, or eye. (Picture yourself having to
   hop on the one remaining foot in order to get to
   where you can repeat a sin.)

There is no substitute for forsaking sin. Many counselees will go through all sorts of exercises, do any other kind of homework that you may propose, avow that they are anxious to change their ways, and yet stop short of forsaking old ways, temptations, and stumbling blocks. Sometimes the counselee does not understand fully how to make the necessary changes. The counselor must be patient; remember that some people learn slowly (II Tim. 4:2). He must explain again, and, if necessary, again and again. Perhaps he has not adequately explained the process in the first place. Or perhaps because of past failure the counselee is hesitant to try again. After all, it hurts to get your hopes up, only to fall flat on your face. The reasons for failure have to be examined meticulously. But what if the failure stems from mere unwillingness?

The judgment that a counselee is stubbornly resisting must be made cautiously. There are any number of reasons why he may be slow to forsake sin. All such possibilities should be explored first before you label a counselee "stubborn." The tendency of some biblically oriented counselors to jump to that conclusion should be balanced by the precaution of judging as one would want himself to be judged (Matt. 7:1ff.).

Still the charge must sometimes be made that a counselee is simply unwilling to forsake sin. Since willingness is the first evidence of genuine repentance, it must be ascertained. Some counselors plough ahead, never knowing for sure whether the counselee is willing. Then, all too often the counselee balks at doing what he is instructed from the Scriptures to do. Better than waiting for resistance and balking is checking on willingness at the outset. When one confesses that he is wrong, agrees with the conviction of his sin and says that he wants to abandon his former ways and develop new, God-pleasing ones, then is the time to check out his commitment to change.

One way to do so is to say something like the following:

> That's great, Mary. I am delighted to hear you say you
> are committed to change. But I wonder if you know
> what that means. People are always talking about com-
> mitment, but no one, it seems, takes the time to spell
> out what it involves. When I say "commitment," I mean
> at least these things: an understanding of what must be
> done, a desire to do whatever God wants, faith that it
> can be done, an ability to do it, and a willingness to set
> aside the time to do it. It also involves persistence or
> perseverance in the face of difficulties. Of course, in all
> of this, we shall be calling upon God for His help. Now,
> let's examine each of those items separately, applying
> them to your case specifically. . . .

Some such thorough check will catch failure to understand or other problems that could be *mistaken* for resistance, as well as uncover genuine resistance itself.

A person's willingness to forsake sin can be gauged in
terms of his self-denial. Jesus taught us that discipleship
means forsaking even good things and persons in order to
follow Him when He said we must "hate" even our loved
ones.[2] He thereby separated the excuse makers, who until
then had avowed allegiance to Him, from those who truly
meant business. When the rich young ruler balked at self-
denial, Jesus would go no further with him. Likewise, if the
homosexual balks at denying himself all future associations
with another homosexual, you will know you are faced with
an unwillingness to part ways with sin.

Such instances call for warnings of the consequences of
resistance. Proverbs 13:15; 28:13; and 29:1 are among the

2. Luke 14:26ff. "Hate" here does not mean having a malevolent
attitude, but, rather, to hate any thing (or person) to stand in the way of
loving Christ. One must go so far as to be willing to hate life itself, if need
be, for Christ's sake.

many verses that could be added to your storehouse and reserved for such times. Persistence in resistance may lead to church discipline.

Perhaps you are wondering, what about those who, in spite of all I have said, are apparently helped by non-biblical counselors. What about those who do not confess sin or follow the biblical process of change, and yet change anyway, seemingly to their benefit? In response to this frequent inquiry (or challenge, as it is often likely to be) let me include my brief editorial that appeared in the *Journal of Pastoral Practice*, 6, 3 (1983): 6, 7:

"BUT . . . IT HELPED"

Occasionally, I hear as the pragmatic objection to my position that counseling must be biblical, and only biblical, "But so and so went to a non-Christian counselor who certainly didn't do biblical counseling, and yet it helped." How does one respond to that protest? Well, by saying that there is help and then there is help.

What I mean by that is that not all help is of the same order, and, in the final analysis, what now may appear to be help—and may actually provide help of a sort—in the long run may turn out to have been more detrimental than good. Smoking will keep one's weight level down—at a terrible cost: cancer. Was it a help or not? Smoking helped keep the weight in check, it is true, but in the long run it did not help—it caused greater and more serious problems. The help it gave was a trade-off. It did not help to enhance the smoker's general welfare. The help carried with it a price that was too high and not necessary for him to pay. Similarly, every instance of "help" afforded by the acceptance and performance of non-Christian principles and practices, in the long run, if not sooner, will reap side effects inimical to Christian living and welfare.

The words "side effects" point immediately to the supposed help of drugs. Insulin and drugs like that are used to supplement bodily output when it is failing to do its job, to help. But any drug that is used, instead of the biblical solution, to mask a problem or eliminate the pains of a person's guilty conscience, in the long run will be found to exact more than double the price he expected to pay:

1. The user probably will become dependent on, if not addicted to, the drug.
2. Over a period of time, the drug will more than likely cause physical injury to the body.
3. The drug may cause troublesome symptoms.
4. The problem will not vanish, but will grow.
5. The person using the drug for such a purpose will not grow stronger for having confronted and solved the problem biblically, but will, in fact, turn out weaker for having avoided doing so.
6. God's solution to the problem will have been ignored and God's blessing withheld.

Was the drug user *helped*?

All sorts of non-Christian counsel may be given ("Take your anger out on the golf ball"; not "learn God's way to control and use anger") that may provide immediate "help" (or, perhaps, in such situations, the word "relief" might better suit the case), but, again, because it isn't God's way to deal with the problem the final results in terms of one's relationship to God, in terms of his personal growth and in terms of what the unbiblical counsel, at length, does to his body and his human relationships, are not worth the price.

So, the answer to the question is "Yes," a help of sorts may be given, but since non-Christian help is not God's help but rather a substitute for it, in the long run (if not sooner) that "help" always will prove to be a detriment.

In contrast, God's help benefits, and does nothing but benefit. Every time a Christian properly avails himself of God's help, not only does he find the help that he seeks, but along with it come side effects that he had not anticipated. This time, however, the side effects are good. Following biblical counsel about anger, for instance (see *Competent to Counsel*), in time will change one's disposition so that he will become a more likeable person and easier to live with.

Now, what will you say to the next objector? Won't you tell him, "There is a help that hurts, that destroys and ruins, and there is a help that truly helps—God's help?" Won't you say, "My help is from the Lord," and tell him that God is a "very present help" in "time of trouble"? You can have the former—I'll take the latter every time; thank you very much.

True success, then, is success as God sees it. And that success requires the forsaking of sin.

Assignment

Examine all of the passages in which Jesus speaks of "denying" (or saying no to) oneself, crucifying one's own desires (taking up the cross daily), and following Him. Write a paper on how you would use these verses in a counseling case in order to help a counselee loosen his grip on sin.

20

Restoration

A frequently neglected but greatly important aspect of forgiveness and correction is the formal reinstatement or restoration of a repentant believer.[1] A great evil in our churches today is that whenever open sin leads to church discipline, the sin is made public but the restoration is not.

This problem begins in the home. Little Johnny and Suzie hear some of the arguments and fights between Mommy and Daddy, but the reconciliation almost always takes place in private. Not only does this lead these little ones to wonder whether matters have been resolved ("Will they erupt again?"), but it also fails to teach them the ways and means of reconciliation. They learn a good bit about the techniques of fighting and expressing anger sinfully (something they might as well be left to develop on their own without such vivid examples!), but they do not learn much about biblical correction and, especially, restoration.

1. There is another side to restoration: the restoration of a wayward, but now repentant, believer to his work of ministry in the body. I have written of this in *Ready to Restore* (Phillipsburg, N.J.: Presbyterian and Reformed Publishing Company, 1981).

Even if it is not always appropriate for the children to witness the actual process of reconciliation, the parents should at least inform the children that a proper relationship has been restored. Perhaps later they could discuss, at least in general, how this was accomplished. How better could children be taught than in such a milieu?

But the problem is not confined to the home. In the church there are all sorts of people who maintain a *de facto* second class status because they have never been formally reconciled or restored to the rest of the body. Having fallen into sin, they either cut themselves off or were cut off from full fellowship, but without formal disciplinary action.[2] Then later, after repentance and perhaps confession and forgiveness, they were more or less restored, though again informally and without public recognition in the church. Others, not privy to the facts of their quasi-renewed status, either are ambivalent about how to relate to them or continue to treat them as deserving of discipline. Because of the muddled handling of the case restoration is never clearly made, and the people in question find themselves relegated to the back of the Sunday school bus.

In such a situation, many in the body will remain confused as to how to relate to a sinning party either before or after his repentance. Perhaps they will not even know that he has sinned or that he is yet unrepentant, and so they fellowship with him as if nothing has happened. They may wonder why others have "grown cold" toward him (and perhaps toward them too). If and when he repents, they will probably learn nothing of it, having not first known of his sin. And, typically, this sad condition stems from the church's failure to take formal disciplinary action (Matt.

2. Sometimes people are cut off even though they are not guilty, e.g., the innocent party of a divorce, in whose congregation any or all divorce is seen as illegitimate.

162   How to Help People Change

18:15ff.) or restore the repentant brother (II Cor. 2). Consequently although members may know something is going on, they are not sure what,[3] and so they are confused about what to do.

A person who has repented of a divorce or some other scandalous (i.e., public) offense and yet has been granted no formal, official restoration may for the rest of his days be regarded with suspicion in his congregation. That is not the biblical way. Where repentance has occurred—even after so heinous a crime as incest (cf. II Cor. 2)—there is need for formal restoration so that the person involved "won't be overwhelmed by too much pain" (v. 7b). And, in such cases, the members of the congregation, alerted to the offender's forgiven and restored status, will not be at a loss about how they should relate to him. Indeed, when the announcement is made that the brother has repented and is forgiven, all should celebrate the return of the prodigal. To encourage such rejoicing, an announcement might well be made that forgiveness and assistance and love are to be shown to him, and that if gossip or shunning follows his restoration, those involved in such unforgiving and unreconciling behavior may themselves become subject to discipline.

How does one go about restoring an offender so that the situation is fully "corrected" and the member is able to "stand up straight again"? The process and procedures of church discipline, including restoration, should be thoroughly understood by all members of Christ's church, especially pastors and elders, and any others who do counseling.

---

3. Uncertainty, in such situations, is fertile breeding ground for gossip, which ultimately may cause more harm than the sin that occasioned it.

Church Discipline

It is because church discipline is not adequately practiced in the Christian church that the above problems exist. The church has been remiss in following the procedures outlined by Jesus Christ in Matthew 18:15ff. and elsewhere in the New Testament. Erasures from rolls, ostracism, lethargic and half-hearted admonition and simple neglect to do anything are substituted for the biblical process. Because I have discussed church discipline elsewhere and because there is now available an excellent series on the subject by Roger Wagner in the *Journal of Pastoral Practice* 6, 1-4,[4] I shall not outline the process in detail here. But let me just emphasize one point in connection with the process that relates directly to correction and, in particular, to restoration.

First, if the first two informal stages of church discipline fail (confrontation one-on-one, and later with one or two additional witnesses), the matter then comes before the officers of the church. If they too are unsuccessful in effecting reconciliation, the matter is officially brought to the attention of the whole church (Matt. 18:17). In such instances, the state of the unrepentant party is formally made known to the entire body so that all may know how to treat him.

The proper manner of relating to him is set forth in II Thessalonians 3:14, 15 and in I Corinthians 5:11. As long as he remains unrepentant, members of the congregation may not treat him as though all were normal. Rather, they are to admonish or counsel him about his sin. They are not to treat him as an unbeliever, however (that follows only upon excommunication), but they must recognize that normal fellowship (symbolized in eating together) is to be

4. Obtainable from the Christian Counseling and Educational Foundation, 1790 E. Willow Grove Ave., Laverock, Pa. 19118.

broken. There should be an official announcement that the brother is unrepentant and is in this third stage of church discipline and that all are called upon to exhort him and pray for him.

Restoration Procedures

If a brother or sister repents after there has been a formal announcement of the disciplinary action, there must also be a formal, official announcement of repentance and forgiveness.[5]

Restoration is clearly explained in II Corinthians 2:6-11, where three requirements are set forth:

1. The repentant brother or sister must be "forgiven."
2. He must be "comforted" (or "assisted"—that is the basic idea in the word *parakaleo*) in whatever ways may be necessary.
3. The church must "reaffirm" its "love" to him. This word "reaffirm," in the original, is a term that speaks of a formal, public action.

Plainly, if discipline is handled properly in the first place, restoration can also be handled properly. The status of a person who is officially and publicly restored by the church is not in doubt: he *stands up straight again*. But the person not dealt with in this biblical fashion will not be considered upright in the eyes of many in the congregation. That is one of the principal reasons why correction must be treated as a matter of great importance. Counselors must understand these things in order to use discipline to the full benefit of those who need it, including their restoration following repentance.

5. A record of this should be made in the elders' minutes for the future protection of the repentant party. Pastors and elders come and go. If no record of repentance is kept, the member may have no way of proving that the church of Christ recognized his repentance and restored him.

Even when discipline has not gone beyond the two informal stages, restoration, though informal, is necessary. Those involved in the informal disciplinary action must reaffirm their love for the repentant brother or sister and thereafter treat him or her as one who stands upright again, having full status.[6] Counselors, who usually enter the picture at the second stage, must be sure to fully restore the repentant party to the place he occupied in their lives before the problem occurred. Upon a counselee's repentance, the counselor should immediately *give* assurances that in his sight nothing stands between the repentant party and himself any longer and that he, for one, intends to act on that basis. Any other parties involved in the counseling session should be encouraged to make a similar reaffirmation of their love.

The counselor must do all he can to help the repentant sinner "stand up straight again." (Such assistance is the basic idea behind the word *parakaleo*, translated "comfort.") The restoration of a believer is so important that unless it occurs the entire course of his future life can be adversely affected.

Assignment

Prepare, for role play in class, five situations in which restoration is needed, and be prepared to show how the counselor might bring it about.

---

6. Indeed, forgiveness—not raising the matter again to him, to others, or to oneself—will soon enable them to drop the "again" in their thinking: they will simply see him as a brother or sister in good standing before God and the church.

PART V

STEP FOUR,
DISCIPLINED TRAINING
IN RIGHTEOUSNESS

21

The Need for Disciplined Training in Righteousness

The words "disciplined training in righteousness" say it all. "Training in righteousness" alone does not. In the *Christian Counselor's New Testament*, which I have been quoting throughout, I have used the word *disciplined* in II Timothy 3:16 because the biblical emphasis in the original Greek word cannot be fully appreciated otherwise. What is in view is not training of just any sort, but training like that of a child.

The word in question is *paideia*, which, for instance, is used by Paul in Ephesians 6:4:

But bring them up with the Lord's [*paideia*] and counsel.

There you see the two-sided nature of child raising: both disciplined training (*paideia*) and counsel (*nouthesia*). This two-sided approach is roughly approximate to what Proverbs 29:15 says about "the rod" and "reproof." Structured discipline (the use of reward and punishment)—i.e., discipline with teeth, discipline that gets the job done—and personal counsel are the two sides of child training, which must be kept in balance. Parents frequently err by neglect-

169

ing one side or the other. The biblical parent will stress both. And like the nurture of a child, biblical counseling too involves both elements.

The Hebrew word for disciplined training is *musar*. This important term, which the Septuagint translates primarily as *paideia*, means instruction by chastening. Gilchrist writes, "From the usage and parallels in the O.T., one must conclude that *yasar* and *musar* denote correction which results in education."[1] The latter term is a derivative of the former. The verbs are used regularly for chastisement and punishment (see Gilchrist, p. 878). The clear identification of the Old Testament concept with the New is found in the well-known passage in Hebrews 12:5-11, where chastisement (or discipline, *paideia*) that is unpleasant when administered is said to result in "the peaceful fruit of righteousness to those who have been trained by it." There *paideia* is plainly said to be painful and is likened to the strenuous exercise that athletes endure (v. 11). Moreover, in the Old Testament quotation discussed by the writer of Hebrews, the word discipline is paralleled with the word for whipping:

> The Lord disciplines those whom He loves, and whips every son that He receives (v. 6).

In the context of that passage, the idea of endurance and perseverance under trial is uppermost in the writer's mind (note vv. 1-4). Likewise discipline is to be "endured" with perseverance for its benefits (see v. 7).

There can be no question, then, about *paideia* in II Timothy 3:16; it can mean nothing less than "disciplined training" in righteousness.[2]

---

1. Harris, Archer, and Waltke, *Theological Wordbook of the Old Testament* (Chicago: Moody Press, 1980), 1:386.

2. Notice how in Heb. 12:11 the result of disciplined training is also said to be the peaceful fruit of *righteousness*.

The Purpose of Training in Counseling

But why is it necessary to do training in righteousness structured in terms of reward and punishment? If a person understands God's requirements, willingly confesses his sin, and is restored to fellowship and service whereby he is carrying his load (Gal. 6:5), what more is necessary? Doesn't Christ give him a clean bill of health after forgiveness? What is this additional burden that Paul places on his back?

Forgiveness buries the guilt of the past,[3] that is true. Paul had no desire to dig up what had been properly laid to rest or to add new burdens. He was concerned about the future. By instructing the counselor to use the Scriptures to train in righteousness those who have been corrected, he was attempting to avert one of the most disheartening burdens a Christian can ever bear—the burden of continual, discouraging failure.

Both in and out of counseling, you run across Christians who have given up. As you speak with them about their lives you soon hear something like this:

> Sure, I would like to be the kind of Christian that you describe and that I read about in the Bible and in Christian biographies. But those people must be supersaints; I've tried time and again to be like them, to do all of the things you hear in sermons and read about in the Bible and in Christian books—but it just doesn't work. I do fine for a couple of weeks, but the first thing you know, there I am again, battling the same old habits and sins. It's like climbing the mountain and reaching the top, only to find myself at the bottom having to climb it all over again. I never seem to make any progress. When I should be moving on to the next mountain in my Chris-

3. See my book, *More Than Redemption,* for a lengthy discussion of forgiveness and its place in counseling.

tian growth, I find myself back at the bottom of the same old mountain I have been up against for years. It seems that I take two steps forward, then two steps back. Maybe Paul and the other supersaints can do these things, but I'm not Paul.

What is the problem? Of course, stunted sanctification can have numerous causes. But a principal problem is a lack of "disciplined training in righteousness."

What this means for counseling is that counselors must recognize that there are four steps and not three in the process of biblical change. Change is not complete until the fourth step is accomplished or at least well on its way. Yet, if there is one failure among Christian counselors who in every other respect are truly biblical, it is the failure to follow through on the fourth step of change. Like their counselees, they are anxious to end counseling, and so they succumb to pressures to stop too soon. After all, a busy counselor is anxious to get on to other tasks, and things may be looking good for this counselee. So why not?

I'll tell you why not: because you don't save time at all; the counselee will be back in a few weeks. Moreover, you set him up for the discouragement of falling flat on his face again. And you tempt him to think that God's way is a failure ("If I'm right back where I was three weeks ago, God's way is only temporary; it doesn't really work"). All this while the counselee has yet to pursue God's way of change, having been shown only the first three steps. God gave the Scriptures for all four purposes, and it is wrong of counselors to look for a short cut to effective change by only doing three-fourths of what God requires.

The fourth step of change is absolutely essential. I cannot overemphasize that fact. It is not enough to put off the old ways, even if one guards against them by radical amputation. There must be an equal and opposite, positive effort to put on new biblical ways in the place of the old ones discarded. One cannot really put off the old without replacing it with the new. In every passage in which we are instructed to put off the old patterns of living (especially Eph. 4 and Col. 3) we are also commanded to put on the new ways of righteousness. The two cannot be separated, as if a person could put off one response pattern and then wait around before developing another. Nature abhors a vacuum, and one pattern or another will necessarily manifest itself. So in response to, say, anger, if one has not yet learned to answer with a soft answer, he will answer in anger.

You can see why the fourth step is integral to the whole process of change, and why neglecting or postponing it can nullify all the good and proper efforts that have gone before. When God gave us the Bible to discipline us in new ways, He knew what He was doing. Those who think they can dispense with this step in counseling, therefore, will fail.

Assignment

From the second half of *The Christian Counselor's Casebook* select three cases in which it is obvious that the counselor must use the Bible skillfully to train his counselees in righteousness.

22

Righteousness: The Goal

When Paul wrote that the Bible is useful for "disciplined training in righteousness," what did he mean by "righteousness," and how is it attained through "disciplined training"? Every biblical counselor should be conversant with these important matters.

The Jews rejected Christ because they thought they were righteous in themselves (Luke 18:9). As Paul put it,

> Out of ignorance of God's righteousness, and by trying to contrive their own, they didn't submit to God's righteousness (Rom. 10:3).

Because there is "none righteous" in himself, and all our supposed righteousness is as "filthy rags," such "righteousness" is unacceptable to God. The only righteousness that God accepts is the perfect righteousness that He Himself has provided for those who believe, the righteousness of Christ (see Rom. 3:22). This righteousness is imputed (or "reckoned") to us when we trust in Jesus Christ as Savior. It is Christ's own perfect record of law keeping attributed to us. When we believe in Him, we are counted as righteous as Christ, as if we had never sinned and instead had kept the entire law throughout our whole lives (see Rom. 4:3,4). This is a righteousness that comes by faith (Rom. 4:5,6, 9,11,13,22).

You may be wondering how righteousness can be said to come through disciplined training, when I've just spoken of a righteousness that comes by faith. There's really no contradiction there. The righteousness of which I have just spoken, the righteousness of God in Christ reckoned to our account by faith (Rom. 5:19), is not the same righteousness that Paul had in mind in II Timothy 3:16, though the two are related. The righteousness of faith referred to in Romans 10:3 as "God's righteousness" is the righteousness of justification, which is attributed to all who believe, the very moment they believe.

"Well, then," you ask, "is the righteousness of II Timothy 3:16 the same as the other righteousness mentioned in Romans 10:3, the righteousness that the Israelites tried to contrive on their own?" No, it is not that "righteousness" either. That was the same as the "righteousness" declared to be "filthy rags" in God's sight (Isa. 64:6). The "righteousness of the Pharisees and others was but an outward conformity that had no inward reality to back it up (Matt. 23:28).

What then is this third righteousness of which Paul writes? It is the righteousness of sanctification. When we were justified by faith, we were *declared* righteous, and the righteousness of Christ was reckoned to us. That was a forensic transaction; it did not *make* us righteous. But in II Timothy 3:16, Paul speaks of an actual righteousness that takes place in our lives, not merely in our standing before the court of heaven.

"But," you ask, "if it is something we do, it is no different from the righteousness of the Israelite who tried to make himself righteous, is it?" Yes, it is quite different. This righteousness of sanctification, like that of justification, is also God's righteousness. In other words, it is not "contrived" by us, but it is produced by God as His Spirit works righteousness in us and by us through His Word.

In the Bible God speaks about two kinds of works in the same way that He speaks about two kinds of faith. Just as there is "dead faith" (James 2:17), there are also "dead works" (Heb. 6:1). We know that these dead works are sinful in God's sight because He says they are works for which one must "repent." They are sinful because they are offered in place of the true or living works that God produces only in and through those who have been justified by living faith.

What Paul commanded in II Timothy 3:16 are not the dead works of Hebrews 6:1, but works that grow out of true faith, of which James speaks so highly. These living works are the evidence of true faith. They are the same as the fruit of the Spirit, the fruit appropriate to repentance, of which I have already spoken.

Such righteous works are God's works because they are produced by Him as His Spirit disciplines His regenerate people in the ways of righteousness, according to His Word. Unlike Israel's "contrived" righteousness and "dead works," which grew out of their own wisdom and strength, and consisted of merely outward conformity to the law, this righteousness flows from a new heart that loves Christ and seeks not its own recognition or self-glorification, but God's pleasure. And even these righteous works, because they are produced not without the aid of the Spirit, must be attributed to faith (Gal. 3:3). They are the fruit of "remaining" in the Vine (Christ), without Whom we can do nothing.

What Is Righteousness?

The New Testament word for righteousness means, literally "rightness." The principal Old Testament word that corresponds to the New Testament word, means "straightness." Righteousness is conformity to God's biblical standard. Jesus wants our righteousness to "exceed" the righteousness of the scribes and the Pharisees (Matt. 5:20), not in quantity, but in quality, in character. Our righteousness must flow from hearts changed by the Spirit, hearts which, under His control, produce His fruit for God's glory.

As we have been counted righteous *in Christ*, so we are now to become righteous *in our actual lives*. In other words, in Ephesians 4 and Colossians 3, when Paul says "you have put off the old person that you were" and "you have put on the new person that you now are," he is but speaking half the truth. He goes on to exhort us to "put off" those same things in daily living that in Christ we are already counted as having put off, and he commands us to "put on" those things in daily living that we are already counted as having put on in Christ. In effect, he says, "Be what you are." In other words, we are to approximate in daily sanctification what is already true of us in Christ through justification. While justification, the declaration of righteousness that comes when we trust Christ as Savior, is an instantaneous, once and for all act, sanctification is an ongoing process by which the Spirit gradually molds us into Christ's image through the Word. This process continues throughout the remainder of our earthly lives and will not be completed until death or the second coming—whichever comes first.

According to Paul's words in II Timothy 3:16, the change of lifestyle called sanctification occurs, at least in part, when we submit in faith and obedience to the "disciplined training in righteousness" provided by the Scriptures. That training will be better understood as we look at the next chapter. But for now, it is crucial to understand that apart from such biblical training, a counselee will fall short of God's righteousness, which is the goal of all Christian living: "Seek first His empire and His righteousness and all of these things will be added to you" (Matt.6:33). Paul looked forward to that day when Jesus Christ would place the "crown of righteousness" on his head (II Tim. 4:8). That crown would be the perfection of his life in total righteousness, so that not only would he be counted righteous in God's sight because of faith, but he would also *be* righteous in every sense of the word. Like Peter, he was looking forward to the new heavens and new earth "in which righteousness will be at home" (II Pet. 3:13b).

Assignment

Write a three-page paper on legalism as a pharisaical perversion of biblical counseling.

23

But Is Righteousness Possible?

Is it really possible to be righteous? To lead a righteous life? To truly please God? Perhaps much of what you read seems to say no. And in your own life you fail frequently. Yet you are told in the Bible that in Christ a Christian is a "new creation." You know you are saved, but there seems to be little growth, little victory over sin. And so you wonder, is it really possible in this life for a Christian to be different after all?

The question is an important one, and every counselor must be certain of its biblical answer.

Emphasize the Upbeat

In Zechariah's prophetic hymn, God predicted deliverance from the power of sin through Jesus Christ. Among other things He declared that Christ's coming is

> making it possible for us to serve Him fearlessly in holiness and righteousness before Him all our days (Luke 1:74b-75).

179

Plainly, God offered reason to think that those who trust in Christ can live righteous lives before Him. The hymn is positive; it puts the emphasis on the hope of a new and different way of life. Christ's coming means change, real change.

In Romans 6:6 Paul wrote,

> . . . our old person was crucified with Him so that the body of sin might be made ineffective, and we might no longer serve sin as its slaves.

And, in Romans 6:14, 18, he continued,

> sin must not be your lord and master; you aren't under the authority of sin but under grace . . . and having been freed from the authority of sin you became slaves of righteousness.

Those two verses make it absolutely plain that we have been emancipated. Sin is no longer our lord, our master. We are no longer helpless, at its mercy, under its power and authority; Christ has freed believers from enslavement to sin. But more than that, those who trust in Him and receive this emancipation in Christ are brought under a new authority: they are made the slaves of a new lord and master (vv. 20, 22):

> When you were slaves of sin, you were free from the authority of righteousness. . . . But now, having been freed from sin, and having become God's slaves, you have the fruit of sanctification for yourselves, and its result is eternal life.

Those words make it clear that we belong to a new master called Righteousness, not the old master, Sin. Under the rule of our new master, we are called to tasks of holiness and righteousness. Contrary to some modern teaching, we are no longer dominatd by sin, unable to live righteously, and stuck in a bumbling, miserable existence of no spiritual growth. That is clear from the teaching of the entire New Testament, particularly the verses we have been citing. A Christian's life can be different, because the believer may now live a life characterized not by sin but by righteousness. Indeed, the figure of the slave master says even more: as his life in the past was ruled and dominated by sin, so now it is ruled and dominated by righteousness. Yes, righteousness is possible.

In I Peter 4:1, 2, similarly we read,

> Therefore, since Christ has suffered in the flesh, arm yourselves also with that thought, because whoever has suffered in the flesh has come to a parting of the ways with sin. As a result, it is now possible to live the remainder of your time in the flesh no longer following human desires[1] but following the will of God.

In this verse Peter says several things: (1) that because of our identification with Christ's substitutionary death in the flesh, the problem of sin in the flesh (described as human desires) has been dealt with; (2) that whenever we face the temptation to sin, there will be a battle (he uses a military term, *arm*, which means to take up one's battle gear); (3) that we are equipped to resist sinful human desires by remembering that in Christ we have died to sin; and (4) that it is therefore possible to live differently for the rest of our lives.[2]

---

1. Not all of our desires are wrong. But we must not follow their leadership. They must be satisfied only when they correspond with the will of God in Scripture and only in the way and to the extent that Scripture allows.

2. See my commentary on I Peter, *Trust and Obey* (Phillipsburg, N.J.: Presbyterian and Reformed Publishing Company, 1978), for details of exegesis, and especially for comments on important connections with contextual material in the third chapter.

It is absolutely essential to understand that righteousness is a definite possibility for the Christian. In this life no one will be perfect, but because of what Christ has done it is now possible to change one's past ways and live differently in the future. What makes the difference in the battle with temptation and sin, in the struggle with human desires, is to recognize this possibility and the reason for it: Christ's death. Peter, here, is saying virtually what Paul said in the beginning of the sixth chapter of Romans. Because we are "in" Christ (i.e., identified "with Christ," so that all He is and all that He did is attributed to us), we are new persons, counted by God to be *like* Him. We are crucified, dead, and buried to all of the old ways; we have been raised to new life and new ways; and we have ascended and are seated in the heavenlies on the right hand of the Father, in Christ.

It is our task, as we saw in the previous chapter, to *become* what we *are*, that is, to become practically what we already are positionally in Christ. The point of these passages that speak of our identification with Christ is not to improve our self-image—there isn't a single hint of the sort[3]—but to assure us that it is possible in daily life to become more and more of what we already are in Christ, and to urge us to do so. Indeed, Paul is amazed that we should do anything else: "How can we who died to sin still live in it?" (Rom. 6:2b).

How does one live differently? How is the righteous life to be carried on? That is the concern of both Peter and Paul, and their first responses are identical: You must count yourselves dead to the past sinful life and alive to future possibilities of living for the honor of Christ (Rom. 6:5-11); arm yourselves with this thought, and you will be able to withstand the enemy (I Pet. 4:1). Both Paul and Peter concen-

---

3. This is the modern psychologizing of the text that we find everywhere in eclectic Christian writers today.

trate, in the first place, upon one's viewpoint.[4]

There has been too much teaching among Christians that would imply, if not say explicitly, that it is virtually impossible for a Christian to live a life that is pleasing to God. While teaching the attainability of sinless perfection in this life would surely be wrong, it is every bit as wrong to resign ourselves to standards and expectations below what God has in mind for us. When counselors foster that outlook, they hinder growth by destroying hope in their counselees.

What I am saying is that there has been an overemphasis upon the continued sinfulness of the Christian. In an attempt to refute erroneous perfectionistic teachings and to keep Christians alert to temptation, some have severely down-played the possibility of gaining real victories in the battle against sin. They have not proclaimed clearly, loudly, or consistently enough that God has made every provision for defeating sin and for spiritual growth. The two sides of the picture must be kept in proper balance. Counselors must encourage counselees with the possibility of overcoming sin, as well as warn them of the possibility of falling into sin. Unless the counselee is made aware that in Christ He is freed from the dominion of sin, is a servant of righteousness, and now has all he needs to live a new way of life, he will not likely put forth the effort required to live as he should. The Scriptures are filled with the hope of victory over sin. They are so upbeat in that regard that they consistently exhort us to prosper in our Christian living as though it is not only possible, but the most natural thing in the world for the Christian to do.

That must also be the counselor's attitude, which he must communicate to his counselee. Peter and Paul make it clear that in order to live properly and struggle successfully against sin, one must have the right outlook. Unless the

4. In the next chapter we shall consider what else must be done.

counselor instills that outlook into the counselee's mind by means of the appropriate scriptural passages, he will be working against attitudes that preclude establishing new patterns of living. The attitude expressed in the opening paragraph of this chapter is all too typical among counselors. Every counselor, therefore, must lay to rest any doubts about the possibility of overcoming the sin or sins with which the counselee is struggling.

Either new patterns are possible or they are not. Every counselor must be clear about this truth and clearly present it to his counselees. He must know, as Peter put it in I Peter 1:18, that

> you [were] set free from the useless behavior patterns that were passed down from your forefathers,

and that John was not talking through his hat when he said,

> Whoever is doing righteousness is righteous as He is righteous (I John 3:7b).

It is possible to "do righteousness" just as Christ did and to develop patterns of behavior that honor God. Every counselor must affirm unmistakably that it is possible to put off wrong patterns of behavior learned from one's parents or culture, and walk in newness of life. Otherwise, he sets his counselee up for failure and discouragement.

For far too long the Christian church has been majoring on the negative side of the Christian life, rather than on the positive. That is why Robert Schuller's shamefully erroneous book on self-esteem can get a hearing. The church itself has plowed the ground for heretical teaching. The answer to the problems of life is not to deny original sin, declare that the Reformation doctrines were wrong, and launch one's own "New Reformation" via unbiblical teaching about self-esteem. The answer is to retain the truths about man's sinful nature and then emphasize the truth that a redeemed man has been set free from the dominion of sin so that he may begin to "do righteousness." No one has any business counseling until he affirms, with John, that it is truly possible for a child of God to "do righteousness."

Notice I did not say that doing righteousness is easy, or that a believer would always do righteousness. Nor did I say that a person who has learned to do righteousness will never slide back into sinful behavior patterns again. All that I am affirming—and it is a large point in itself—is that it is possible for a Christian to follow Christ, as His disciple, walking in righteousness. Not perfectly, not completely, but nevertheless truly. This every counselor must affirm.

That means that the homosexual truly can put off his sinful way of life and adopt instead a sexual lifestyle that is pleasing to God. It means that the drunkard can lay aside his habit and become a sober man. It means the thief, the gossip, the liar can all put away those lifestyles and adopt alternative patterns of life that honor God. That is what the Scriptures themselves teach in I Corinthians 6:9-11. Here were people whose lifestyles were so characterized by such sins that the people themselves were described in terms of the sin. Yet, by the power of the Spirit, through His Word ministered by His servants, the people were able to put their sinful ways behind them and live righteously: "such *were* some of you" (v. 11).

Romans 7

"But what about Romans 7?" you ask. "Doesn't Paul in that chapter concede defeat to the evil within? And what is that evil within? Can you explain more clearly what chapters 6–8 of Romans are all about?"

That is a large task, one that cannot be fully undertaken in this book. I hope some day to do a thorough exegetical study of those three chapters in relation to the Christian life. Here, I can make only a few suggestions.

First of all, let us say that Roman 7:14ff. is the record of a Christian and his struggle with sin, not the struggle of an unbeliever. And it does not represent a Christian who is wrongly handling his sin either; the experience here is the experience of every believer. (It is not worth arguing the issue with anyone who claims he is not acquainted with the problem in his own experience. He would be too insensitive to understand the apostle as he reveals his heart of hearts. One wonders how he could be sensitive enough to minister to others in counseling.)

We have seen that a believer is reckoned perfect in Christ. And it is abundantly clear both from Scripture and from experience (I John 1:8, 10) that he is not perfect in daily life.[5] We have also seen that all he is in Christ he is commanded to be also in daily living. Moreover, we are told that he is equipped with everything necessary to grow into the stature of Christ (cf. Heb. 13:20, 21). Those are established points so far.

But how can believers, who are "new creations" and have new hearts of flesh that replace the hearts of stone (Ezek. 36:26), yet sin? How can they be freed from the old master, Sin, be enlisted in the service of Righteousness, and yet not do all that they ought? In short, how can they say with Paul, ". . . whenever I want to do a fine thing, I am aware of evil" (Rom. 7:21b) and, "What I want to do I don't practice, but instead what I hate is exactly what I do" (v. 15b)? And, finally, how can a Christian cry out with sorrow and remorse, "What a miserable person I am! Who will rescue me from this body of death?" (v. 24).

He can do so because, although he is counted perfect in

5. On I John 3:9, see the footnote in Horatius Bonar, *God's Way of Holiness* (Chicago: Moody Press, n.d.), p. 99.

Christ, he is not yet perfect in himself. The Christian is not a consistently faithful slave of Righteousness; he is in the learning process. There is sin yet in his life. But it is precisely because he has a new outlook on life, serves a new master, and desires to do the will of the Lord, that his failure to please God becomes a matter of sorrow and remorse. As an unbeliever he would hardly be overwhelmed by his sin. But, because he has a new orientation and the Spirit dwells within him, he is concerned and distressed over his short-comings.

The believer especially comes to grips with his remaining sin as he struggles with sin in his body. Writer after writer tries to avoid the all-too-obvious fact that in chapters 6–8 Paul spoke about the struggle he had with his body. They say that when Paul used the word *body* he referred to the part as standing for the whole. Similarly, the word *flesh* is made over into *sinful nature* (cf. the NIV, where these very words are used instead of *flesh;* the NIV is very loose and not an adequate study Bible, though valuable as a commentary). And often they ignore the plain and unmistakable words about sin *in the bodily members.* Speaking about the same experience we all know, Paul was describing a body that often acts contrary to one's mind. Failure to recognize that has kept counselors from helping many people with what is a universal problem.

"But," you may wonder, "if Paul is speaking about the body, doesn't that involve Christianity in the errors of Greek mind-body dualism?" Not at all. The body is never considered sinful in itself in the Scriptures as it was in Greek philosophy, which called it the prison house of the soul. The body is respected and will even be resurrected. To understand *body, members,* and *flesh* to be speaking of the actual body, and not something else, is to take the words at their face value. Paul was not speaking of the body as sinful in itself. But the body is the locus of a problem.

Before Paul became a Christian, he habituated his body to sinful patterns of living by yielding its members to sin, which led to more sin, and taught the body (including the brain) the very sinful responses he later came to deplore (to return evil for evil, for instance). Because he indulged the body's desires in various sinful ways, it became habituated to them so that after conversion it was inclined to do what it had always done before. Paul was reaping the fruit of what he had sown in his body. It had been organized against what he as a Christian wanted to do. He was struggling against his own programing (both his conscious sin and others into which he drifted, as do all sinners).

But the great truth is that the Holy Spirit has come to repattern and remold that body as well as the soul. It is an important though neglected truth that the body is being sanctified, as well as the soul (see I Thess. 5:23; I Cor. 6:20).[6] And it is most instructive to learn that the members of the body can be yielded to Righteousness, the new master to whom the redeemed belong.

So this struggle of Paul in Romans 7 does not always end in defeat; victory over bodily temptation and rebellion is always possible.[7] That is what we are being told throughout. The wonderful fact is that the habituation of the brain and the rest of the body which it controls can be changed now that there is a new impulse in the soul and there is life for understanding, believing, and desiring what God's Word requires. Romans 8 tells that happier story.

To walk in the flesh is to walk in the old ways (the old man = the old lifestyle). This body is so organized by sinful

6. See Louis Berkhof, *Systematic Theology* (Grand Rapids: Eerdmans Publishing Co., 1945), p. 533.

7. Paul is not conceding defeat in Rom. 7; he is admitting to a struggle, the outcome of which, regrettably, is not always victory.

patterning that it is like carrying around a weight, dead to the things of God. That is why Paul called it a "body of death" (7:24). Moreover, he repeated this in Romans 8:10, where he said that the body is dead (spiritually) because of sin. But, as Calvin rightly teaches, concerning verse 11, Paul rejoiced that the Spirit of God gives life to those "mortal bodies" as well:

> We hence conclude, that he speaks not of the last resurrection, which shall be in a moment, but of the continued working of the Spirit.

That is why Paul continued, writing in verse 13,

> But if by the Spirit you put to death your bodily practices, you will live.

Thus, the new heart in man, enlightened and strengthened by the Holy Spirit, who dwells within, is in the process of changing and remaking the whole man—including this body, which so stubbornly reacts against what we want to do. There is great hope for change, then, because there is hope even for the change of the habituated body. Though at times it seems a body of death, that death itself can be put to death so that the body begins to live for and serve Righteousness. This happens as one yields his members to Righteousness.

And it is particularly this yielding of the bodily members, presenting them as a living, acceptable sacrifice to God (Rom. 12:1, 2), that we shall be examining as we look more closely into the disciplined training in righteousness that the Word of God provides.

Assignment

In a brief paper, list as many sinful habit patterns as you can that will need to be put off, together with the biblical alternatives by which they must be replaced.

24

Biblical Training

We have said that the first factor in disciplined training in righteousness is to recognize that change is possible. Hope of truly replacing sinful ways with righteous ones is essential for both the counselor and the counselee. Without it the counselee will not persevere in the face of the struggles with sin that lie ahead. He must "arm" himself with the thought that since he is "in Christ," identified with Him, he too has "come to a parting of the ways with sin" (I Pet. 4:1). He must believe that there is the possibility of living the rest of his days differently than in the past (I Pet. 4:2). The counselor must have the same hope too. Otherwise he will convey his own hopelessness to the counselee—the last thing an uncertain counselee needs![1] And the counselor must believe that change is possible not only to communicate hope to doubtful counselees, but also because the process of change can be discouraging to counselors, as well as to counselees. So, the first matter of importance is to believe that people whose lives have been steeped in sin can change.

If you do not believe that, you should not counsel. It is

1. Counselees are quite adept at picking up counselor attitudes.

one of the basic tenets of our Christian faith that God saves
and changes people. If, like many in the church today, Paul
thought that people can never get very far from their early
training and habits, he surely would not have written as he
did to the converts in the churches at Corinth, Thessalonica,
and elsewhere. Those letters certainly recognize problems,
but the problems are dealt with, and change is expected.
Paul accepted no excuses for bad living patterns; if after
reasonable amounts of instruction, exhortation, and other
help (*paraklesis*) the convert does not shape up, discipline
awaits him. It is not being hard on a believer to expect him
or her to change. Indeed, it is the most encouraging attitude
that one can take. It declares that change is not only possible
and righteousness is not only available; it is expected—or
else!

We have also seen that there are two ways to look at a
regenerate person: from the perspective of what he is in
Christ and from the perspective of what he is in daily living.
And the former, the perfection of righteousness that by
faith is counted or reckoned to be ours in Christ, becomes
the standard for what by faith and living works we must
become in daily living. We are to become (in daily living)
what we already are (in Christ).

In Christ	*In Daily Living*
This is our position, legal status, or standing before God as Judge.	This is our actual state or condition in daily life before God as our Father.
We are sanctified once for all and counted perfect because of the righteousness of Christ which is attributed to us.	We are being sanctified day by day as the Spirit of God, through the Word, enables us to become more like Christ.

This work is finished, complete, and unchangeable.	This work is continuing and incomplete, and change is occurring.
We are forgiven, once for all, judicially.	We are being forgiven day by day, parentally.
We are totally freed from sin, doing nothing but righteousness.	We are freed from sin's dominion and capable of doing righteousness.

With these facts in mind, let us turn now to a consideration of the training in righteousness that the Scriptures provide. We have seen that the New Testament term for "disciplined training in righteousness" as well as its Old Testament counterpart, is related to the education of children and carries the idea of reward and (especially) enforcement of learning by punishment or chastisement. That is to say, such training has teeth; it is calculated to get results. Unlike much of the training that goes on today, which amounts to a take-it-or-leave-it offering of data, biblical training is intent on achieving its goals. In other words, the emphasis is not on the instructor putting in his time, but on the trainee acquiring certain desired information and lifestyle skills.

This training consists of learning the biblical alternatives to the acts, attitudes, and lifestyles that need to be replaced. It consists of "putting on" the new man (new ways) in place of the "old man" (old ways). There is no possibility of putting off unless there is an equal and concomitant putting on. Thus, when the thief is told to put off stealing, he is instructed to develop patterns of hard work and giving (Eph. 4:28), and the liar is required to replace habits of lying with habits of truth telling (v. 25). It is not enough to stop stealing or to quit lying, as some think. The process of change is two-factored. Unless the new ways are learned, the old ones will reappear. The person may "break" a pattern or habit temporarily, but he will resume it once again if he has not learned a new one to take its place. That is to say, the body (which, remember, includes the brain) must be reprogramed. Counseling works with this reprograming to effect the fourth step of change.

Habit is an important factor and deserves more attention in theology and Christian counseling. In the Bible it plays the same important part it does in everyday living. A large share of what we do day by day is by habit. The Bible recognizes that and gives habit its rightful place.

Habit is a blessing from God that enables us to do things unconsciously, automatically, skillfully, and comfortably (its four characteristics) so that we can do other things at the same time. But as sinners we have perverted this blessing and, like other God-given capacities (e.g., sex), we have often turned it into a curse. Counselors must learn the power of habit, the importance of habit, how to eliminate sinful habits, and how to establish new righteous ones.

Because I have dealt with habit, dehabituation and rehabituation, and the biblical putting off and putting on dynamic in depth in *The Christian Counselor's Manual*, I will not replicate that work here. I simply refer you to it. Instead, I wish to take up some related matters that have not yet been adequately set forth.

Training Deals with Habit

Biblical training is not concerned with intellectual instruction alone.[2] One of the great difficulties with our educational system in Western society is that we all too frequently train people not for personal change, but for the ability to pass tests. There is, of course, some change in a person when he studies for a test. But the goal of training *for righteousness* is quite different, as is therefore the product of such training. When your goal is to mold the character of an individual, you pursue that task much differently than when your goal is to enable him to answer questions. That is why counselors must deal not merely with intellectual information—transmitted, learned, and fed back—but also with habit. Paul's habits were what caused his struggle. Your task as a counselor, who is engaged not merely in teaching facts, but in changing people so that they pursue righteous living, is to learn to use Scripture to replace sinful habits and lifestyles with biblical ones.

One of the important considerations we have been addressing throughout this book is change that occurs on the outside alone, with no foundation in the heart. Obviously, there are plenty of self-help experts and behavioral engineers who will contract to change you—on the outside. But that will not do; pharisaism is not pleasing to God. He wants hearts that are aligned to Him and to His purposes. He wants the change on the outside to flow from and be a part of an inner change aimed at pleasing Him. So an important consideration is whether the dehabituation-rehabituation process is pursued as a gimmick or as a means of pleasing God. If, of course, the other three steps have been followed for the right reasons, then the counselee's attitude upon entering the rehabituation process ought to be proper. Yet, before proceeding, you would always be wise to impress upon the counselee the need for aligning

2. The Great (Educational) Commission: ". . . teaching them to *observe*" (Matt. 28:20). Truth must lead to godliness.

both heart and action with the will of God.

Moreover, dealing with habits must be viewed as the work of the Spirit through His Word, not the work of the counselee, or the counselor and the counselee alone. It is not as though "the Spirit has done His work of convicting and leading to confession, and now it is up to us to do ours." What changes us is the Word ministered in the power of the Spirit—He is at work in His Word throughout the entire four-step process. Therefore, the counselor must stress that even in the formation of new patterns, he and the counselee must call on the Spirit to make clear what the new patterns must be; and to strengthen and assist them in learning to follow the new ways. The counselor sets an example for the counselee by the things he says, by his dependence on the Spirit through prayer, and by the hope he exhibits in relying on the Spirit and the Word to make the change.

Another matter concerns the four characteristics of habit mentioned above: a habit involves unconscious, automatic, comfortable, and skillful action. Because both counselees and counselors are often anxious to end counseling, new patterns may fail to be established. As I have mentioned earlier, one or the other (or both) is ready to quit too soon. It is important not only that the counselee learn how to guard against future failure through radical amputation, as well as learn what to do in place of the old sinful response, but also that the counselor be sure that the new habit patterns are becoming established before counseling is terminated. If he doesn't stay with the counselee long enough for him to establish these patterns, then he will doubtless have the work to do all over again.

How may he know when to bring counseling to an end? In the *Christian Counselor's Wordbook*, I have listed some general criteria for determining when counseling should terminate (see "Termination of Counseling").[3] But here, specifically, let me add that a good test is to look for the four characteristics of habit as they begin to occur. Until the counselee has begun to develop the new patterns adequately enough for them to become more or less automatic, unconscious, comfortable, and skillfully performed, he must not terminate counseling. The wise counselor will want to see evidence of these factors.

It is not always necessary for this process to have developed to the full, but only for the patterns of the new lifestyle to have begun to take on these four characteristics. If the other terminating criteria have been met, the counselor may schedule the next session as a "six-week checkup" and allow time for the full maturing process to occur.[4] If all goes well, in six weeks the new pattern should be habituated. Simple experience has shown that it takes about 40 days (and 40 nights?) to establish a new pattern. So, if you have worked on the habit for 3 or 4 weeks during counseling and begin to see the four signs of rehabituation appear with frequency, allowing another six weeks for it to fully mature will give it more than ample time. In some cases you may want to call the counselee back for a three-week checkup instead.

Another factor that should be mentioned in regard to rehabituation is coaching. Call it what you will, but in various passages relating to habit formation, the Bible uses athletic imagery, thus my choice of the word *coaching*. The coach is concerned not only for his players to become rehabituated to new actions but for them to become *properly* rehabituated. He is concerned that from the beginning they

3. *The Language of Counseling and the Christian Counselor's Wordbook* (Grand Rapids: Zondervan Publishing House, 1986), p. 87.
4. It is wise, whenever possible, to enlist and instruct a third party to check up on the counselee weekly during this period.

learn to perform exactly as they should. Counselors some-times settle for too little—less than a football coach or a piano teacher would.

The good coach stays especially close to the trainee in the early goings. He sets up a heavy structure designed to avert bad habits by correcting even slight deviations from the pattern he wants the trainee to learn. In short, he will not allow the trainee to develop sloppy habits. He is zealous for precise performance and will accept nothing less. Should counselors settle for less than a piano teacher or a football coach?

This concern for learning things right the first time is important. You can see how what might seem to be a minor deviation can, in the long run, become a major problem for the counselee. Indeed, counselors will discover, to every-one's chagrin, that when they have settled for less than what is biblically correct, they only have to redo the whole process later, this time breaking down habits that they themselves allowed the counselee to develop. What a trag-edy!

Counselors should recognize that counselees are prone to do the wrong thing unless they are heavily coached at the beginning. As the counselee begins to get the hang of it, the counselor then backs off and lets him develop skill on his own. But from the very beginning, the counselor should fully explain the reason for the close supervision. We have nothing to hide; there is nothing esoteric about Christian counseling; it should not be done in a corner. Even before the counselee asks, we should recognize the need to explain our procedures and anticipate his questions. Not only will understanding the rationale behind your methods make it easier to get compliance and cooperation, but it will also allay concerns and will inspire confidence that you know what you are doing. So, whenever any action on your part is likely to arouse questions, it is wise to anticipate and take the initiative to explain.

Habit is very much a part of our lives, yet, because of its characteristics—being unconscious, automatic, comfortable, skillfully executed—the average person may not be aware of how vital a part it plays in day to day activity. Habits simply don't call attention to themselves. You can demonstrate that from your counselees' own statements: "I didn't realize I was raising my voice to my wife when I said that." "Do you mean to tell me that when I speak to my husband I actually have a scowl on my face?" You should go on to demonstrate how much of our lives depend on habitual responses. You might say something like this:

> Have you ever realized how much you would be hampered by the elimination of all of your habits? Imagine waking up tomorrow with no habits at all. There you lie, wondering what to do next. "I guess I should get up," you tell yourself. But then comes the decision about how to do it. Do you jump out with both feet or throw one over the side of the bed first? Which one, and over which side? Then there is the problem of brushing your teeth—unscrewing the top on the tube of toothpaste (no easy job for one who has no skill in doing it: watch your child learning), squeezing the paste onto the brush, rather than your hand or the sink, and, of course, brushing. I won't even mention the many other difficulties with ablutions, putting on your shirt, buttoning it, tying shoelaces, and so on. Why, you'd be doing well to get to breakfast by midnight! And, in addition to all of these ordinary, simple tasks, think of trying to drive a car, making decisions, dealing with nasty people, etc. No, you cannot escape the fact that without habit you would be at sea. So you can see how important a part habit plays—unconsciously—in your life. That is why the Bible requires us to deal with it.

Paul said,,

> You were taught regarding your previous habit patterns
> to put off the old person that you were, who is cor-
> rupted by deceitful desires . . . (Eph. 4:22).

That should make us sit up and take notice. Paul was saying
that his readers, after being converted to Christ, were taught
about putting off the old ways and (in the verses following)
putting on the new ones. Today new converts are taught no
such thing. That is one of the major reasons why they seek
counseling for such problems only months or years later.
They need not, indeed must not, wait that long. They can
begin replacing old habit patterns right away, because, as
the next verse (v. 23) indicates, the new convert is being
rejuvenated in the attitude of his mind. The word for re-
juvenate or renew means to "make youthful again," and
youthful attitudes, growing out of study of the Word illumined by the Spirit, provide the ideal condition for
change.

The word that I have translated as "habit patterns" in
the *Christian Counselor's New Testament*, which I have been
quoting, is *anastrophe*, a term that means "a habitual manner of life." It approximates Paul's other term, used in the
last three chapters of Ephesians (and shared by John in his
writings), meaning "walk." Both words indicate a habitual
lifestyle. Habit is also plainly referred to in I Corinthians 8:7;
15:33; and Hebrews 5:14. This last passage notes the importance of regular practice in developing habits. The idea
of developing godliness through discipline has been fully
explained in a booklet of the same title, *Godliness through
Discipline*.[5]

Clearly habit and its place in counseling is important,

5. Phillipsburg, N.J.: Presbyterian and Reformed Publishing Company, 1972.

particularly in disciplined training in righteousness. What I have said about habit here, I would remind you, is minimal and supplementary; my full treatment of the subject is already well known, and it would be useless merely to replicate that material here.

Assignment

Because of the importance of habit in counseling, particularly in the fourth step of change, read the pertinent chapters in *The Christian Counselor's Manual* and write a one-page synopsis of what you read.

25

Conclusion

Some years ago, at a conference in the Pinsgau Valley of Austria, a fellow speaker made an astounding statement to the effect that

> Whenever I don't have time to study my Bible to find the answer to a question, I just ask God to give me the answer in a dream. Then I find that Jung's principles of dream analysis come in handy.

I call this statement astounding because he was the head of an evangelical student movement in one of the European countries and should have known better. With this sort of thing being taught to students, it is no wonder you find people confused and needing help. When I countered his statement, telling him that the only source of revelation from God by which we can expect to be guided in this life is the Scriptures, he persisted in affirming that dreams and various other means of revelation were just as viable.

That is probably the greatest difficulty we who believe the Bible have to face today—people turning to substitutes for the Scriptures. You will meet counselees who depend upon hunches, saying that the Spirit "prompted" them, or else that He "checked" them "in the spirit" (both of which boil down to following feelings). You will meet people who "put out the fleece" (and who usually keep putting it out till they get the answer they desire!). You will meet those who try to interpret "circumstances" not altogether unlike the way the ancients did augury with chicken livers or the way a modern-day Gypsy reads tea leaves. But when you do, you will also meet confused, mixed up people whose methods of solving problems have only compounded the messes they are in.

One of the most important things you can do when counseling others, then, is to make clear that the sole source of information and guidance that you will follow in counseling is the written, inspired Word of the living God, which is useful to make all of the necessary changes.

At times you will have to argue that point. But generally your counseling itself should demonstrate that the Bible has the answers to human problems, and that, when properly used, it provides the practical solutions to the exigencies of life. Throughout, one of the major ways to help your counselees, therefore, is to show them how practically to use the Bible (for more on this, see my book, *What to Do on Thursday*).

I cannot exhort you strongly enough to remain ever mindful of the usefulness of the Bible for changing Christians. It will do the job, if only given the opportunity. But if it is used sparingly and superficially, the results likewise will be sparse and shallow. The Christian counselor must be a workman in the Word who handles it accurately as he interprets it, analyzes his counselee's problems according to its categories, and shows God's application of its truth to the counselee's life. So used, the Bible will prove to be more than you could ever ask or think. You will be amazed at how the Spirit of the living God uses His Word to solve even the most stubborn and resistant problems and to triumph over the most difficult circumstances. If you don't believe me, try it. Why not lay aside for six months all of the other techniques, principles, and systems you have been using with, at best, mixed results, and concentrate on using the Bible alone? To do so takes earnest effort and time to learn both how to launder your mind of pagan psychological and psychiatric theories and how to use the Bible cogently and effectively in its full strength. In all of this you must ask the Spirit of God to sustain and guide you, by the Bible, of course! If you do, I can assure you, from the testimony of hundreds of others who have, that you will never look back to the weak and beggarly elements again. You will have reason, yourself, to thank God that His Word can bring about such a change.

The Christian Counselor's Casebook
Applying the Principles of Nouthetic Counseling
Jay E. Adams

This companion volume to *Competent to Counsel* and *The Christian Counselor's Manual* is designed to help the user assimilate and apply the principles of nouthetic counseling. It is an excellent tool for any Christian counselor who is striving to develop a scriptural approach to counseling. Because it is a workbook based upon actual counseling experiences, the cases are  typical of the variety of problems according to biblical norms, practice in laying out biblical plans of action, and familiarity with a variety of types of problems. By working through the many cases provided, the counselor will be better able to identify and respond to the issues that typically confront Christian counselors. This is not merely a book for the classroom; it is a tool for all sorts of training and personal development programs.

Softcover
ISBN: 0-310-51161-5

Pick up a copy today at your favorite bookstore!

ZONDERVAN™
GRAND RAPIDS, MICHIGAN 49530 USA
WWW.ZONDERVAN.COM

The Christian Counselor's Manual
The Practice of Nouthetic Counseling
Jay E. Adams

The Christian Counselor's Manual is a companion and sequel volume to the author's influential *Competent to Counsel*. It takes the approach of nouthetic counseling introduced in the earlier volume and applies it to a wide range of issues, topics, and techniques in counseling:
- Who is qualified to be a counselor?
- How can counselees change?
- How does the Holy Spirit work?
- What role does hope play?
- What is the function of language?
- How do we ask the right questions?
- What often lies behind depression?
- How do we deal with anger?
- What is schizophrenia?

These and hundreds more questions are answered in this comprehensive resource for the Christian counselor. A full set of indexes, a detailed table of contents, and a full complement of diagrams and forms make this one of the best reference books currently available for Christian counselors.

Jacketed Hardcover
ISBN: 0-310-51150-X

Pick up a copy today at your favorite bookstore!

ZONDERVAN™

GRAND RAPIDS, MICHIGAN 49530 USA

WWW.ZONDERVAN.COM

We want to hear from you. Please send your comments about this
book to us in care of the address below. Thank you.

GRAND RAPIDS, MICHIGAN 49530 USA

WWW.ZONDERVAN.COM